D0112600

Meet the real Jesus

Meet the real Jesus

John Blanchard

Foreword by John F. MacArthur Jr

 **EVANGELICAL PRESS**

EVANGELICAL PRESS
Faverdale North Industrial Estate, Darlington, DL3 0PH, England

Evangelical Press USA
PO Box 825, Webster,NY 14580, USA

e-mail: sales@evangelicalpress.org
web: http://www.evangelicalpress.org

First published 1989
Second impression 1989
Third impression 1989
Reset 2001

British Library Cataloguing in Publication Data available

ISBN 0 85234 258 6

Other books by John Blanchard

How to enjoy your Bible	Ultimate questions
Pop goes the gospel	What in the world is a Christian?
Read Mark Learn	Does God believe in atheists?
Right with God	Invitation to live
Whatever happened to hell?	The man who made the millennium

Affectionately dedicated to my five sons

Christopher John
Timothy James
Andrew David
Stephen Paul
Michael Peter

Contents

Foreword

Here is the kind of book we need more of! It is simple without being simplistic, and doctrinally rich without sounding dull and dry. Best of all, it persuasively presents the truth about Jesus Christ in such a coherent way that nobody who reads it can possibly miss its message.

Here is communication *par excellence*. John Blanchard has given us one of those rare books which will be of value both to the sceptic and to the person who is already convinced about the truths it reveals. Not only is it a richly rewarding study of 'the real Jesus', it is an impressive apologetic for the truth and historicity of the Bible. As such, it will strengthen the faith of the believer and authoritatively challenge everyone else's unbelief.

John Blanchard supplies a wealth of factual and doctrinal information in thoroughly understandable terms, and his approach is a refreshing contrast to the trifling form of gospel presentation that has gained popularity in our time. Here the subject is treated with comprehensive authority. Anyone who rejects what this book has to say will not be turning away in ignorance; and anyone who responds positively will have solid ground for his faith, rather than the shallow emotional footing which so much modern treatment of the subject tends to produce.

If you are reading this book as someone who genuinely wants to discover 'the real Jesus', I urge you to give it your serious and objective attention. What you are about to discover will introduce you to the most important person you can ever know. What you do with him has implications for all eternity.

John F. MacArthur Jr
Sun City
California

1.

The man in sixty billion

By the time you have finished reading this chapter about another 400 human beings will have been born. Even allowing for the current average death rate, the world population of six billion is increasing by over 70,000 a day, over 2,000,000 a month, and more than twenty-five million a year. Estimates of the total number of human beings who have ever lived on our planet are in the order of sixty billion.

The many, the few and the one

Of those billions, the overwhelming majority have lived and died virtually unknown, leaving little but their names. Some have done more — their work, teaching or example trailing a few temporary ripples behind them. Others — not nearly so many — have a greater claim to our attention: their achievements have affected thousands, even millions of people. Finally there have been comparatively few who have had a major effect on human history. Philosophers, scientists, rulers, politicians and founders of religious movements are among those on this select list. Some of them have become world-famous and are household names, with their influence (good or bad) reaching deeply into the lives of millions of people all over the world.

Yet in that élite group there is one person who stands out from all the rest. No other human being in history has attracted such a combination of attention, devotion, criticism, adoration and opposition. Every recorded word he spoke has been studied and sifted, analysed and scrutinized by generations of theologians, philosophers and others. Every one of his recorded actions has attracted the same intense interest. Today, twenty centuries after his death, there is never a single moment in which less than several million people are reading what he said and did and trying to apply the significance of his words and actions to their lives. That person is Jesus — sometimes known as Jesus of Nazareth — who lived about 2,000 years ago.

Facts are facts

This preoccupation with Jesus becomes even more amazing when we put certain facts alongside each other.

- Nobody knows the exact date of his birth, but that one event divides the whole of world history into the years labelled 'B.C.' (before Christ) and 'A.D.' (from the Latin *Anno Domini*, meaning 'in the year of the Lord').[1]
- He never wrote a book, but more books have been written about him than about anyone else in history. The nearest thing we have to his biography — the part of the Bible called the New Testament — has been translated in whole or in part into over 2,000 languages.
- He never painted a picture or composed any poetry or music, but nobody's life and teaching has been the subject of a greater output of songs, plays, poetry, pictures, films, videos and other art forms.
- He never raised an army, but millions of people have laid down their lives in his cause. It has been calculated that every year the almost unbelievable number of 330,000 of his followers are martyred for their faith.[2]

- Except for one brief period during his childhood, his travels were limited to an area the size of Wales,[3] but today his influence is literally worldwide.

- He never spoke to more than a few thousand people at any one time, but today his followers constitute the largest religious grouping the world has ever known.[4]

- His public teaching lasted only three years and was restricted to one tiny country, but today some of the world's largest radio and television networks are given over exclusively to spreading his words, while purpose-built communication satellites are positioned in space to carry his message around the globe.

- He set foot in only two countries, but one Christian missionary organization[5] claims to fly regularly to more countries now than any commercial airline in the world.

- He had no formal education, but thousands of universities, seminaries, colleges and schools have been founded in his name.

- He never owned any property; he had to borrow a boat to sail in, a donkey to ride on, and even a coin to use for an illustration, but all around the world today thousands of buildings have been erected for the sole purpose of teaching his followers and adding to their number.

- In his own lifetime he was relatively unknown outside of his own tiny country, but in the current edition of *Encyclopaedia Britannica* the entry on 'Jesus' runs to nearly 30,000 words.

Media man

When we bring all of these facts together it is not surprising to find the noted historian Kenneth Scott Latourette saying that 'Jesus, the seeming failure, has had more effect upon the history of mankind than any other of its race who has ever existed.'[6]

Man's interest in Jesus seems to be insatiable. In spite of hundreds of earlier volumes on the same theme, it has been estimated that between 1910 and 1950 some 350 books on the life of Jesus were published in the English language alone.[7] Since then, the output has accelerated; in the six years from 1968 to 1973 more books about Jesus were published than in the previous fifty.[8]

More recently, Jesus has invaded other mass media. The stage show *Godspell* became an instant smash hit. So did *Jesus Christ Superstar*, which went on to become the longest-running musical in the history of the London theatre. In the nineteen-seventies the Italian film producer Franco Zeffirelli's film *Jesus of Nazareth* took the cinema-going world by storm. It was seen by nearly 90% of the Italian viewing public within a few years and now counts its total viewing figures in hundreds of millions. Another film, simply called *Jesus* and based directly on his re-corded words, has been produced in over 100 languages and has already been seen by more people than any other film in history.

The real Jesus?

But who is (or was) Jesus? There is the traditional view (and we shall come to that later) and an almost endless list of mangled or watered-down versions of it. Then there are those who speak of Jesus the political revolutionary, Jesus the religious *guru*, Jesus the mystic and Jesus the faith healer. Others have come up with much wilder speculations. In 1970 philologist John Allegro suggested that far from being a historical figure Jesus was no more than the code-word for an ancient sex-cult inspired by a hallucinogenic mushroom. This did not enhance his academic reputation, and in the words of one critic 'gave mushrooms a bad name'! Allegro died in 1988; his hypothesis did not survive him. In 1984 London Weekend Television screened a three-part programme called *Jesus — The Evidence* (in which they had invested two years and nearly £400,000) and came up with a ragbag of theories including those suggesting that Jesus was a hypnotist, an occultist, a magician and a sexual deviant. In their book *The Holy Blood and the Holy Grail*, M. Bagient, R. Leigh and H. Lincoln put forward the novel notions that Jesus was an intergalactic freedom fighter who came to earth and married, and that his descendants are secretly plotting to take over Europe!

You may think that some of these ideas are far-fetched and others downright ridiculous. But even if you dismiss them all, the obvious question still needs to be answered: '*Who is the real Jesus?*'

2.

The man who was here

But are we going too fast? Perhaps the first question we should be asking is not 'Who is the real Jesus?' but 'Is there a real Jesus?' Did such a person ever exist, or is he nothing more than a myth invented by eccentric and religious fanatics? The question is hardly irrelevant; if he has no historical basis, all other questions about him would tend to fall a bit flat!

Who says so?

Virtually all the contemporary written evidence about Jesus comes from the Bible, which we will examine shortly. In the meantime, what other data do we have? Not much — but enough!

The most important witness is Flavius Josephus, who had a meteoric career in the first century as a student, priest, military commander, diplomat and historian, and has been described as 'perhaps the most distinguished and learned Jew of his day'.[1] His real name was Joseph ben-Matthias but he adopted the family name of the Roman Emperors Vespasian and Titus. His most famous work is *Antiquities of the Jews*, twenty volumes which tell the story of his people from the creation to the fall of Masada in A.D. 66. In one of these Josephus writes about social unrest in Judea during the time when Pontius Pilate was the Roman procurator there (A.D. 26-36) and includes this paragraph: 'Now, there was about this time Jesus, a wise man; for he was a doer of wonderful works, a teacher of such men as receive the truth with pleasure. He drew over to him both many of the Jews and many of the Gentiles. And when Pilate, at the suggestion of the principal men among us, had condemned him to the cross, those that loved him at the first ceased not so to do; and the race of Christians, so named from him, are not extinct even now.'[2]

Notice how many *facts* are included: Jesus is said to be a wise man, a miracle-worker and a teacher, to have been crucified on the instructions of Pontius Pilate and to be the founder of a 'race' of people called 'Christians'.

Josephus also records that in A.D. 62 a Jewish high priest called Annas was sacked because he illegally convened the Sanhedrin (the Jewish ruling council) 'and brought before them the brother of Jesus the so-called "Messiah"[3] who was called James, and some other men, whom he accused of having broken the law, and handed them over to be stoned'.[4] As historians agree that James was stoned to death in A.D. 62, the mention of Jesus is an important piece of evidence — and as it is mentioned only in passing, it is even more impressive.

The second witness is Suetonius, official historian of the Roman Empire's Imperial House. When rioting broke out in the large Jewish community in Rome in A.D. 49, the Emperor Claudius banished all Jews from the city. In the words of Suetonius, 'He expelled the Jews from Rome, on account of the riots in which they were constantly indulging, at the instigation of Chrestus.'[5] Nobody suggests that Chrestus (a misspelling of 'Christ')[6] was ever in Rome in person; it was the introduction of his spiritually radical teaching into the traditionally Jewish community that caused such commotion. Nevertheless, the reference to the historical Jesus is clear.

Next comes Cornelius Tacitus, the Roman Governor of Asia, another distinguished historian (and the son-in-law of Julius Agricola, who was Governor of Britain from A.D. 80-84). When the Emperor Nero was suspected of starting the great fire which devastated Rome in A.D. 64 he quickly tried to blame others. Tacitus tells us that 'To dispel the rumour, Nero substituted as culprits, and treated with the most extreme punishments, some people, popularly known as Christians, whose disgraceful activities were notorious. The originator of that name, Christus, had been executed when Tiberius was emperor by order of the procurator Pontius Pilate.'[7] Again, notice the historical checkpoints linking Jesus to the life and times of Tiberius (Caesar Tiberius, who was Roman Emperor from A.D. 14-37), and Pontius Pilate (who was procurator of Judea from A.D. 26-36).

Our fourth witness is Plinius Secondus ('Pliny the Younger') who was a contemporary of both Tacitus and Suetonius. Pliny was appointed Governor of Bithynia (now part of Turkey) by Emperor Trajan about A.D. 111. Pliny has been described as 'one of the world's great letter-writers, whose letters ... have attained the status of literary classics'.[8] He was in the habit of writing to Trajan for advice, and one such issue concerned the correct way to punish the growing number of Christians in his area. Pliny reports that his practice was pretty straightforward: 'I have asked the accused themselves if they were Christians; if they said "Yes", I asked them a second and third time, warning them of the penalty; if they persisted I ordered them to be led off to execution.'[9] And what was their 'crime'? 'They were in the habit of meeting on a certain fixed day before sunrise and reciting an antiphonal hymn to Christ as God, and binding themselves with an oath — not to commit any crime, but to abstain from all acts of theft, robbery and adultery, from breaches of faith, from repudiating a trust when called upon to honour it.'[10] This powerful piece of evidence shows that at an early stage there were already growing numbers of people who believed in

the historicity of Jesus and who were so committed to his radically high standards of moral behaviour that they were prepared
to die for his cause.

Finally there is Lucian, a second-century satirist who ridiculed Christianity and described Jesus as 'the man who was
crucified in Palestine because he introduced this new cult into
the world'.[11]

So much for the evidence outside of the Bible.[12] It may not
seem much, but we need to bear in mind that very little literature from that time has survived and that historians seeking to
record the major events in those days would hardly be expected
to devote reams of writing to a penniless peasant from a scruffy
little town in a remote part of one of the world's smallest countries. What *is* significant about the evidence is that it comes
from people strongly *opposed* to Christianity. They did not have
a good word to say for it (although Pliny was impressed by the
lives of Christians) yet they wrote openly of the life and death
of Jesus as historical events. In his paperback *Beyond the
Gospels*, Roderic Dunkerley examines all the available contemporary evidence outside of the New Testament and comes to
this conclusion: 'In none of these various testimonies to the fact
of Christ is there any slightest hint that he was not a real historical person.'[13]

Why believe the Bible?

So far, we have been trying to see whether contemporary historians said anything about Jesus, but when we turn to the
Bible, which teems with evidence about him, the question becomes 'Can we rely on what it says?' In his *Introduction to
Research in English Literary History*, military historian C. Sand-
ers lays down three tests for assessing the reliability of ancient
documents. The first is the *bibliographical test,* which asks

questions like these: How many manuscripts (handwritten copies) do we have? How good are they? How close in time are they to the original (or 'autograph' as it is called)? The second is the *external evidence test*, which asks whether there are other contemporary sources to confirm the statements of the document in question. The third is the *internal evidence test*, which asks whether the original author was writing truth or error, fact or fiction. That is a pretty thorough examination! How does the Bible perform?

Let me interrupt myself at this point. If you have no problem in accepting the Bible's reliability and trustworthiness, you might want to ignore the rest of this chapter and go straight to chapter 3. You can always come back to this chapter later as a refresher course on the material it contains.

The message of the manuscripts

First of all we will put the Bible through the *bibliographical test*. We need to do this because we no longer possess any of the original documents forming the basis of the sixty-six books we now call the Bible. That seems to torpedo its credibility straight away — but beware of jumping to conclusions! Look at the first question the bibliographical test asks: how many manuscripts of the New Testament documents do we have?[14] Amazingly, we have no fewer than 20,000, each containing all or part of the New Testament — a very impressive total when we look at other ancient documents. For example, we have only nine or ten copies of Caesar's *Gallic War* (58-50 B.C.) and just twenty copies of Livy's *Roman History* (59 B.C. – A.D. 17). The material we have from the great works of Tacitus depends entirely on just two manuscripts. We have seven copies of the histories written by Pliny the Younger, eight copies of the works of Suetonius and nothing we can completely trust about Alexander the Great, even though many books have been written about him. No other ancient document approaches the New Testament's weight of evidence; the runner-up to its 20,000 manuscripts is Homer's famous *Iliad*, and that has only 643.

This leads to the second question: how good are these copies? At first glance, the answer seems ominous because there are about 200,000 differences (or 'variants' as they are called) in the documents. But this figure is very misleading. For example, one misspelling in 3,000 different manuscripts is counted as 3,000 variants — and the number can quickly be whittled down further. Drs Norman L. Geisler and William E. Nix have stated that the 200,000 variants are confined to 10,000 places,[15] while another expert, Philip Schaff, has pointed out that only 400 variants could have any possible effect on the meaning of the passage involved, and that only fifty of these are of any importance.[16] He also went on to say that not one of these changes a single article of faith or duty which is not 'abundantly sustained by other and undoubted passages, or by the whole tenor of Scripture teaching'.[17]

How do other ancient documents compare? Very badly! Even Homer's *Iliad* (the runner-up in the manuscript count) has twenty times the number of instances where the original words are in doubt. Sir Frederic Kenyon, one-time director and principal librarian of the British Museum, put it like this: 'It cannot be too strongly asserted that in substance *the text of the Bible is certain: especially is this the case with the New Testament*. The number of manuscripts of the New Testament, of early translations from it, and of quotations from it in the oldest writers in the church, is so large that it is practically certain that the true reading of every doubtful passage is preserved in some one or other of these ancient authorities. *This can be said of no other ancient book in the world.*'[18]

Now to the third part of the bibliographical test. How close in time are the earliest manuscripts to the original documents?

Again, the off-the-cuff answer sounds pretty depressing. The earliest part of any biblical document we have is the *John Rylands Fragment*, a scrap of papyrus[19] measuring two and a half inches by three and a half inches and presently housed in the John Rylands Library, Manchester. It contains five verses from the eighteenth chapter of the Gospel of John and is thought to date from A.D. 117-138. Next comes the *Bodmer Papyri*, a collection of documents including a copy of the Gospel of John from about A.D. 200, an incomplete copy of the Gospel of Luke from about the same date and a third-century copy of three other New Testament books, 1 Peter, 2 Peter and Jude. Scholars put the same kind of date on the *Chester Beatty Papyri*, which contain most of the New Testament.

Then come the oldest major manuscripts. The first of these is the *Codex Vaticanus*,[20] with seventy-six papyri manuscripts containing fourth-century copies of almost the entire Bible, and which has been stored in the Vatican library for over 400 years. The second is the *Codex Sinaiticus*, which contains over half of the Old Testament and all but twenty-four verses of the New Testament and, like the *Codex Vaticanus*, is dated around A.D. 350. From then on the trickle becomes a stream, which rapidly widens into a flood of 20,000 documents. Yet we have to concede that the earliest major New Testament manuscripts are dated about 350 years after the events they claim to record.

That seems a gigantic gap — until we compare it with the time-lag involved in other ancient documents. The earliest surviving manuscript of Caesar's *Gallic War* is dated A.D. 900, some 1,000 years after the original. Livy's *Roman History* has only one fragment less than 400 years distant; the works by Tacitus show a gap of over 700 years, the histories of Pliny the Younger 750 years and the work of Suetonius 800 years. Once more, the New Testament has no serious rival. As Sir Frederic Kenyon puts it, 'In no other case is the interval of time between the composition of the book and the date of the earliest extant manuscripts so short as in that of the New Testament ... and the last foundation for any doubt that the Scriptures have come down to us substantially as they were written has now been removed. *Both the authenticity and the general integrity of the books of the New Testament may be regarded as finally established.*'[21]

The voice of history

We now turn to the *external evidence test*. Are there other contemporary sources to confirm the Bible's statements? Yes there are. The earliest comes from the famous Jewish historian Eusebius, who was born about A.D. 263 and preserved the writings of Papias, a personal friend of the apostle John, one of the New Testament authors. Papias reports John as saying that 'Mark,[22] having become the interpreter of Peter, wrote down accurately all that he [Peter] remembered, whether sayings or doings of Christ... So Mark made no mistake, writing down in this way some things as he [Peter] mentioned them; for he paid attention to this one thing, not to omit anything that he had heard, nor to include any false statement among them.'[23]

Then there is Irenaeus, who was a student of Polycarp, a disciple of the apostle John. Writing around A.D. 180, Irenaeus says this: 'Matthew published his Gospel among the Hebrews[24] in their own tongue, when Peter and Paul were preaching the gospel in Rome and founding the church there. After their departure[25] Mark, the disciple and interpreter of Peter, himself handed down to us in writing the substance of Peter's preaching. Luke, the follower of Paul, set down in a book the gospel preached by his teacher. Then John, the disciple of the Lord, who also leaned on his breast[26] himself produced his Gospel, while he was living at Ephesus in Asia.'[27] Those words are electrifying! They come from the friend of a friend of one of the original authors of the New Testament. No wonder that Irenaeus writes elsewhere of having the preaching of the apostles still echoing in his ears and their doctrine in front of his eyes. It would be unreasonable to expect to get closer than that! In fact, the authenticity of the New Testament writings was so firmly established and so widely accepted in Irenaeus' day that even those who were spreading false doctrine quoted from them in order to give their own twisted teaching some semblance of credibility. As Irenaeus put it, 'So firm is the ground upon which these Gospels rest that the very heretics themselves bear witness to them.'[28]

Call Sir William Ramsay

The other major piece of external evidence is provided by archaeology. Years of painstaking work have gone into unearthing the records of ancient civilizations in the Middle East, and one of the by-products has been the opportunity of comparing the archaeologists' discoveries with the biblical records. One of the world's most brilliant archaeologists was Sir William Ramsay (1851-1939). Professor of Classical Art and Architecture at Oxford University, Regius Professor of Humanity[29] at Aberdeen University, founder member of the British Academy, holder of nine honorary doctorates from universities in Great Britain, Europe and America, and knighted in 1906 for his distinguished service to the world of scholarship, his credentials as a witness are pretty impressive!

Ramsay was trained to believe that the New Testament narratives were largely myths, and that reverent imagination had wrapped the real truth in stories invented many years later. Ramsay was convinced, for example, that the Acts of the Apostles was written not by Luke but by someone else about 100 years afterwards. When he began some archaeological studies in Western Turkey (part of 'Asia' in New Testament language) he was sure that his work would destroy the credibility of the New Testament narratives once and for all, but his theories soon came unstuck. His problems began in 1910 when he made a major discovery about the exact location of the city of Iconium which proved Luke right and later historians wrong. The further he went, the more the Bible was vindicated. In his own words, 'It was gradually borne upon me that in various details the narrative showed marvellous truth.'[30] The book in which he wrote these words, *St Paul the Traveller and Roman Citizen*, hit the world of biblical criticism like a bombshell, but Ramsay was not finished yet. As he pursued his studies the evidence he unearthed totally convinced him that not only did Luke write Acts but that he was no ordinary writer: 'Luke is a historian of the first rank; not merely are his statements of fact trustworthy, he is possessed of the true historic sense ... in short, *this author should be placed along with the very greatest of historians*.'[31] This assessment was later echoed by Professor E. M. Blaiklock, Professor of Classics at Auckland University, New Zealand: 'Luke is a consummate historian, to be ranked in his own right with the great writers of the Greeks.'[32]

That accumulated evidence in this area is now so powerful that the eminent Jewish archaeologist Nelson Glueck has no hesitation in saying this: 'It may be stated categorically that *no archaeological discovery has ever controverted a biblical reference*.'[33] The New Testament passes the external evidence test with flying colours, and people dismissing it as 'a load of rubbish' — often without having read it — can be safely ignored.

The book that speaks for itself

We now come to the *internal evidence test*, which asks whether the writers were telling the truth in matters which cannot be corroborated by external evidence. This is a massive question, and requires massive qualifications on the part of the person who dares to answer it off his own bat. Think of the great *variety* of material contained in the Bible, which was written by some forty different authors at intervals stretching over 1,500 years. Professor F. F. Bruce, Emeritus Professor at the University of Manchester, has summarized it like this: 'The writers wrote in various lands, from Italy in the west to Mesopotamia and possibly Persia in the east. The writers themselves were a heterogeneous number of people, not only separated from each other by hundreds of years and hundreds of miles, but belonging to the most diverse walks of life. In their ranks we have kings, herdsmen, soldiers, legislators, fishermen, statesmen, courtiers, priests and prophets, a tent-making rabbi and a Gentile physician, not to speak of others of whom we know nothing apart from the writings they have left us. The writings themselves belong to a great variety of literary types. They include history, law (civil, criminal, ethical, ritual, sanitary), religious poetry, didactic treatises, lyric poetry, parable and allegory, biography, personal correspondence, personal memoirs and diaries, in addition to the distinctively biblical types of prophecy and apocalyptic.'[34]

But that is only the beginning of the critic's problems. Anybody who attempts to prove the Bible wrong requires an expert knowledge of the three biblical languages (Hebrew, Greek and Aramaic), a clear understanding of the context in which each book was written and an intimate knowledge of the circumstances being addressed in each case. He must also be able to identify each author's use of language: was he employing a simile, a localized idiom, metaphor, hyperbole? Was he telling a story as an allegory, a parable, a factual narrative? Even more importantly, was he writing history or prophecy? The critic must also be a master of all the civil law of every country and generation represented in the Bible, and of all the religious and civil customs of every country and age covered by the Bible's writers. Granted all of this, an insight into any other possible shades of meaning which each author may have intended and *all available knowledge of the subject matter concerned*, and the would-be Bible destroyer is ready to start. We will assume a smattering of arrogance!

But my italics are intended to bypass other issues and to focus attention on one crucial fact — that the Bible's overall subject is not Middle East history, nor even the religious history of one particular nation; nor is it a textbook on morals and ethics (though its moral teaching is the finest the world has ever known). Put very simply, *the Bible is about God and his relationship with man* — and no honest, intelligent and wise critic can claim to be an authority in this area. The subject is beyond the scope of any human being.

Words of men or Word of God?

There is one final thing to be said about the Bible's internal evidence — the most important thing of all: it claims to be not the words of men but the Word of God. As you read the Bible this comes across with stunning force. In the Old Testament alone phrases like 'God said', 'God spoke', and 'the word of the Lord came' occur nearly 4,000 times — 700 times in the first five books and forty times in one chapter. Hundreds of years later the apostle Paul claimed, 'All Scripture[35] is God-breathed' (2 Timothy 3:16). The apostle Peter took exactly the same line, saying that in the Old Testament 'prophecy never had its origin in the will of man, but men spoke from God as they were carried along by the Holy Spirit' (2 Peter 1:21).

What is more, the New Testament writers made similar claims for their own writings. The apostle Paul challenged potential critics: 'If anybody thinks he is a prophet or spiritually gifted, let him acknowledge that what I am writing to you is the Lord's command' (1 Corinthians 14:37). Later, he rejoiced that people received his message 'not as the word of men, but as it actually is, the word of God' (1 Thessalonians 2:13). Can you imagine any preacher or teacher today making such an unblinking claim like that about everything he wrote? The apostle John was equally adamant, and said that his writing was nothing less than 'the word of God' (Revelation 1:2) and given to him by 'the Lord, the God of the spirits of the prophets' (Revelation 22:6). The apostle Peter was just as clear and said that he and his colleagues 'preached the gospel ... by the Holy Spirit sent from heaven' (1 Peter 1:12). Nor must we forget that these writers had nothing to gain by circulating forgeries; in fact, many of them were called upon to die for their convictions.

Professor Harold Lindsell sums up the claims of the New Testament writers in this way: 'No one can read any part of the New Testament without being impressed by the fact that the writers convey the sense of divine authority, manifest the badge of truthfulness, and give no impression whatsoever that what they wrote, or what the other apostles wrote, should or could be doubted by the reader. And no writer gives the impression that what he writes is not to be taken as though it came from the very lips of God himself.'[36] The American scholar B. B. Warfield once said that to try to deny that the Bible claimed to be the Word of God by explaining away a text or two (at least to our satisfaction) was like trying to avoid an avalanche by dodging individual stones![37]

To put this another way, the Bible claims to be not speculation by man but revelation by God. Not only is it reliable but it speaks with absolute and final *authority*. (I appreciate that this carries us far beyond the point at which we began to examine the Bible's integrity with a view to proving the existence of Jesus, but our investigation inevitably leads here because of the extraordinary claims the Bible makes about itself.) Someone may argue: 'But surely to claim that the Bible is true because the Bible says it is true, and that the Bible is the Word of God because the Bible says it is the Word of God is to argue in circles?' In a way, it is; as Professor John Frame admits, 'The God of Scripture tells us in Scripture to go to Scripture!'[38] But if God is the author of the Bible where else could he tell us to go? The doctrine of the authority (and therefore, inevitably, the accuracy) of the Bible is one of the Bible's own doctrines. As Robert Horn puts it in the title of his book on the subject, the Bible is *The Book that speaks for itself*: and when it speaks it claims to be the living word of the living God.

Accepting the evidence

There is no way of denying the clarity of the Bible's internal evidence — but will the reader accept it? On this point three things need to be said. The first is that ever since the Greek philosopher Aristotle laid it down over 2,000 years ago, literary experts have accepted his principle that the benefit of the doubt is to be given to the document under examination, and not claimed by the critic. Let the critic probe and press and question with all the legitimate apparatus at his disposal, but in areas of doubt he should be prepared to let the author speak for himself. That seems perfectly reasonable, but some of today's Bible critics give the impression that the only people with no right to make a contribution to the debate are the original authors! When we let the Bible speak for itself its writers testify to its divine authorship, reliability and authority.

The second thing to say is that the acceptance of evidence as *proof* presupposes what John Young has called 'the willingness of the investigator to be open to the conclusions to which the facts point'.[39] Surely no honest seeker after truth can object to that? Where, then, does the evidence point? In the course of this chapter we have subjected Scripture to the tests of bibliography, external evidence and internal evidence, but we could have gone much farther. We have not even touched on its staggering record in the field of prophecy, nor on its impressive unity, nor on its amazing moral, ethical and spiritual influence over thousands of years in the lives of millions of people. Yet no amount of evidence will convince someone who does not want to be convinced; after all, the Flat Earth Society still has an enthusiastic membership. To reject the Bible's reliability falls into the same blindfolded category.

The third point goes beyond the scope of this chapter, but must be mentioned. Ultimately, accepting the divine *authority* of Scripture (which is much more than agreeing that its historical data are accurate) is not a matter of argument but of faith. This must be the case: what other 'machinery' can a man use for accepting the claims of a book to speak infallibly about the nature of God, the nature of man and their relationship to one another? The doctrine of divine revelation means that only God can illuminate the mind and heart of the reader so that that person comes to accept the Bible's reliability and submit to its divine authority. Writing as one who had come to that position, John Calvin put it like this: 'Enlightened by him,[40] we no longer believe, either on our own judgement or that of others, that the Scriptures are from God; but, in a way superior to human judgement, feel perfectly assured — as much so as if we beheld the divine image visibly impressed on it — that it came to us, by the instrumentality of men, from the very mouth of God.'[41]

That is where the Bible rests its case, and it must be accepted on its own terms. External evidence from contemporary literature and archaeology can supply impressive confirmation of the Bible's accuracy in many areas — and should lead an honest enquirer to be open to its central message — but no external material can add anything to the Bible's own unique and remarkable claims.

To get back to the question...

We began this chapter by asking, 'Did Jesus ever exist?' Can there really be any honest doubt about the answer to that question? Writing in *The New Bible Dictionary*, Dr J. N. Geldenhuys makes this important comment: 'In the early centuries A.D. not even the bitterest enemies of Christianity had any idea of denying that Jesus lived and died in Palestine, and that he performed wonderful works, whatever account they might give of the power by which he performed them. Nor at the present day does any objective historian deny the historical fact of Christ. *It is not historians who toy with the fantasy of a Christ-myth.*'[42] Nor do any honest thinkers. As the scientific genius Albert Einstein once said in an interview, 'No man can deny the fact that Jesus existed.'[43]

Does anybody seriously question the existence of Tiberius, Herod the Great or Pontius Pilate (who were contemporaries of Jesus), or Confucius, Alexander the Great or Plato (who lived long before him)? Professor Clark Pinnock is right when he says that, applied elsewhere, the criticism which suggests that Jesus was a figment of men's imagination 'would reduce every historical figure to a puff of wind'.[44] Anybody who denies that Jesus of Nazareth lived on this earth about 2,000 years ago has forfeited the right to be taken seriously.

The real Jesus

Having established the *historicity* of Jesus, we can now get back to our investigation of his *identity*. The very question tells us that there is more to Jesus than meets the eye. Like many great figures in history, Jesus is controversial — but the controversy does not centre around his ideals or moral teaching. Nor can anybody honestly point an accusing finger at the quality of his life. In fact, some of his most glowing commendations come from his greatest enemies.

Here are just three, all from the nineteenth century. John Stuart Mill, a political economist strongly opposed to Christianity, spoke of Jesus as being 'in the very first rank of men of sublime genius of whom our species can boast. When this preeminent genius is combined with the qualities of probably the greatest moral reformer and martyr to that mission who ever existed upon earth, religion cannot be said to have made a bad choice in pitching upon this man as the ideal representative and guide of humanity.'[45] The French humanist Ernest Renan said of Jesus, 'His beauty is eternal ... Jesus is in every respect unique and nothing can be compared with him.'[46] David Friedrich Strauss, a German theologian who tried to tear the New Testament narratives to ribbons, conceded that Jesus 'remains the highest model of religion within the reach of our thought'.[47]

Who was he?

Then why the controversy? It was sparked off by the things that Jesus said and did, but these led to a more fundamental question: *who exactly was he?* This was the question that constantly surrounded him. When Jesus attended the Feast of Tabernacles at Jerusalem, the gossips soon gathered: 'Among the crowds there was widespread whispering about him. Some said, "He is a good man." Others replied, "No, he deceives the people"' (John 7:12). After he had spoken to the crowds the discussion turned to deeper issues: 'On hearing his words, some of the people said, "Surely this man is the Prophet."[48] Others said, "He is the Christ." Still others asked, "How can the Christ come from Galilee? Does not the Scripture say that the Christ will come from David's family and from Bethlehem, the town where

David lived?" Thus the people were divided because of Jesus'
(John 7:40-43).

Later he healed a man who had been blind from birth. The
Pharisees (local religious leaders) were very impressed, but they
were far from unanimous as to the source of his power: 'Some
of the Pharisees said, "This man is not from God, for he does
not keep the Sabbath." But others asked, "How can a sinner
do such miraculous signs?" So they were divided' (John 9:16).
Another part of his teaching brought this reaction: 'At these
words the Jews were again divided. Many of them said, "He is
demon-possessed and raving mad. Why listen to him?" But
others said, "These are not the sayings of a man possessed by
a demon. Can a demon open the eyes of the blind?"' (John
10:19-21). On one occasion a crowd yelled at him, 'You are
demon-possessed' (John 7:20); on another, people cried out,
'Truly, you are the Son of God' (Matthew 14:33). He was worshipped by some, hated by others; he was accused of being a
glutton and a drunkard, and praised for being a prophet and a
king; some said he was demented, others that he was divine.

The controversy still rages today. The modern fires were given
a particularly hefty stoke in the nineteen-thirties by the German
theologian Rudolph Bultmann, who wrote, 'I indeed think that
we can know almost nothing concerning the life and personality of Jesus, since the early Christian sources show no interest
in either, and are moreover fragmentary and often legendary.'[49]
In other words, he was saying because the New Testament
records were written much later than supposed, and by men
who 'invented' the kind of Jesus they wanted others to accept,
we should get rid of these 'myths' and put our trust in 'the
Christ of faith'. But consistent biblical scholars have made pretty
short shrift of that. As Dr I. Howard Marshall puts it, 'A view
which in effect jettisons half the evidence before it can make
any headway is surely in danger of sinking.'[50] To believe with
Bultmann that huge chunks of the New Testament are only

religious fairy tales hardly helps towards an understanding of
what it is saying! One is reminded of the story of the boys who
met to play football, only to discover that nobody had brought
a ball. 'Never mind the ball,' one of the lads shouted, 'let's get
on with the game'! People like Bultmann seem to be saying,
'Never mind Jesus, let's get on with Christianity.' Nothing could
be more absurd. It has been said that 'Christianity is Christ';
what is certain is that you cannot have one without the other.

With all this as background, we can now turn our full attention to our original question. I have deliberately taken time to
establish the accuracy, reliability and authority of the Bible so
that from now on we can allow the biblical evidence to speak
for itself about the most remarkable human being in history.

Saint or sinner? Christ or crank? Messiah or madman? Demented or divine? Who is the *real* Jesus?

3.

The man who was expected

For obvious reasons, almost our entire search for the real Jesus is being conducted within the pages of the New Testament, but the Old Testament also provides some vital data. For the Jews, the Old Testament was not just a record of the nation's history, or a collection of religious writings. Certain groups of scholars (the Pharisees and the Sadducees, for instance) took different lines of interpretation in some areas, but all agreed that the Scriptures were God's Word to his people. So did Jesus. He quoted from them often, and always as the authoritative and infallible 'word of God' (John 10:35).

Neither did the Jews see the Old Testament as a collection of unrelated writings. Instead, it had one great, unifying theme — God's dealings with their nation as his 'chosen people' and with mankind at large. Central to all of this was the promise that one day God would break into history by sending a great deliverer — the Messiah — who would meet man's deepest need and establish the kingdom of God. One prophet after another spoke of his coming, with the last of them, Malachi, summing up God's promise by assuring Israel that 'The messenger of the covenant, whom you desire, will come' (Malachi 3:1). That was God's last word on the subject for 400 years.

The promise and the person

Then Jesus came on the scene. One day, as he was worshipping in his local synagogue, he was invited to read from the
Scriptures. This is what happened next:

'The scroll of the prophet Isaiah was handed to him. Un-
rolling it, he found the place where it is written:

"The Spirit of the Lord is on me,
  because he has anointed me
  to preach the good news to the poor.
He has sent me to proclaim freedom for the prisoners
  and recovery of sight for the blind,
to release the oppressed,
  to proclaim the year of the Lord's favour."

Then he rolled up the scroll, gave it back to the attendant
and sat down' (Luke 4:17-20).

Interesting! This meant that the young man — a local car-
penter's son who was establishing quite a reputation for himself
as a teacher elsewhere — was not content with reading the
Scriptures: he was going to preach. Luke's words capture the
atmosphere perfectly: 'The eyes of everyone in the synagogue
were fastened on him' (Luke 4:20). You could have heard a pin
drop! What would he say? Would he give a dreary repetition of
general principles they already knew backwards or mouth pious
platitudes about 'pie in the sky when you die'? Not a bit of it!
His first words were electrifying: 'Today this scripture is fulfilled
in your hearing' (Luke 4:21). The inference was inescapable:
Jesus was claiming that when Isaiah wrote about the Messiah
he was writing about him.

For all the shock waves that his words must have caused, the initial reaction seems to have been favourable, but as Jesus developed his theme and pressed home some of its implications, the atmosphere turned sour. Eventually the people got so angry they bundled him out of the synagogue and tried to throw him over a cliff. As far as we know, he never returned to Nazareth.

The incident in the synagogue is particularly 'atmospheric', but it was not the only occasion when Jesus made similar claims, drawing as he did so on all three sections of the Old Testament — the law, the poetical books and the prophets. The Jews looked on Moses as the great lawgiver (though they were somewhat selective when it came to obeying his instructions!). On one occasion, Jesus told them point-blank, 'If you believed Moses, you would believe me, for he wrote about me' (John 5:46). The Psalms are the best known of the poetical books and contain many references to the Messiah. Jesus had no hesitation in saying that when he was being persecuted it was in fulfilment of the psalm in which the Messiah says, 'They hated me without reason' (John 15:25). Daniel, one of the prophets, foresees the great deliverer as 'one like a son of man' (Daniel 7:13). And Jesus applied the title 'Son of man' to himself no fewer than seventy-eight times.

There is similar evidence in the Gospels, and one incident will be sufficient to show the *extent* of Jesus' claim. Speaking to a group of religious leaders one day, he commended them for their study of the Old Testament and then condemned them for failing to see its meaning: 'You diligently study the Scriptures because you think that by them you possess eternal life. *These are the Scriptures that testify about me,* and yet you refuse to come to me to have life' (John 5:39-40). That must have been another 'atmospheric' moment, because there could have been no doubt about what he meant — all the Old Testament writers were pointing forward to *him*. The message was clear and confident, but was it correct? Finding the answer to that question will obviously be a major step forward.

The best way to begin our investigation will be to trace the Messianic prophecies back to their roots. Although there are earlier statements, we can begin with Abraham, who lived about 2,000 years before Jesus was born and was called by God to leave his hometown of Ur (probably in what is now southern Iraq) to lead his family to an undisclosed destination. The whole project was an exercise in faith, but in the course of calling him, God promised Abraham that 'all peoples on earth will be blessed through you' (Genesis 12:3). Nearly fifty years later he confirmed this by telling him that 'through your offspring all nations on earth will be blessed' (Genesis 22:18). Here is our first clear reference point: the Messiah would come through Abraham's descendants. This means that 2,000 years before Jesus was born, every other family on earth except Abraham's was out of the running as far as producing the Messiah was concerned.

From Abraham to David

Abraham had two sons: first Ishmael, then Isaac. The line of succession was usually through the oldest son, but in this case God decreed that the promise made to Abraham would be fulfilled through Isaac, not Ishmael: 'It is through *Isaac* that your offspring will be reckoned' (Genesis 21:12). Isaac also had two sons, the twins Esau and Jacob. Esau was a few moments older than Jacob, and technically the firstborn and heir, but again God overruled convention and confirmed to the younger son *Jacob* the promise made to his grandfather Abraham: 'All peoples on earth will be blessed through you and your offspring' (Genesis 28:14).

So far the odds in each case have been no more than fifty-fifty, but now they increase dramatically, because Jacob had twelve sons, the founders of the twelve tribes of Israel. Of these, God bypassed eleven and chose Judah: 'The sceptre will not depart from *Judah* ... until *he* comes' (Genesis 49:10). Eleven generations later (with the odds increasing all the time) we come to a man called *Jesse*. There is no record of God making the Messianic promise directly to him, but several hundred years later the prophet Isaiah brought this word from God:

'A shoot will come up from the stump of *Jesse*;
    from his roots a Branch will bear fruit.
The Spirit of the LORD will rest on him...'
                                                    (Isaiah 11:1).

Now we can follow the line more closely again, because Jesse had eight sons and of these *David* was chosen to continue the Messianic line of succession: '"The days are coming," declares the LORD, "when I will raise up to David a righteous Branch"' (Jeremiah 23:5). Jesus was not born until nearly thirty generations later, and the detailed genealogies were destroyed during the sacking of Jerusalem in A.D. 70, but the opening verses of Matthew's Gospel trace his family back to all the Messianic roots we have just examined. So does the genealogy of Mary, his mother, recorded in Luke's Gospel. (Some people are confused by the fact that the Bible contains two genealogies of Jesus, but a simple explanation would be that whereas Luke records the human descent of Jesus, Matthew records the descent of the crown of David. As the descent of the crown did not necessarily go to the firstborn in the house of David it would follow a different 'line' from that of Jesus' physical descent.)

   To sum up, the Messiah would have to come from a line taken directly through Abraham, Jacob, Judah, Jesse and David — which precludes most of the human race. But we can add two further pointers. One of the prophecies we noted said, 'The sceptre will not depart from Judah ... until he comes' (Genesis 49:10). In other words, Judah would continue to provide Israel with its kings until the Messiah came. As we know that Judah's government collapsed with the destruction of Jerusalem in A.D. 70, Jesus arrived on the scene just before the deadline expired. The second pointer is the Old Testament's prophecy of the town where Jesus would be born: 'But you, Bethlehem Ephrathah, though you are small among the clans of Judah, out of you will come for me one who will be ruler over Israel' (Micah 5:2). There were two Bethlehems, one in the region of Ephrathah in Judea and the other seventy miles to the north, in Zebulon. The prophecy is precise: the Messiah would be born in the first of these; and the New Testament tells us that 'Jesus was born in Bethlehem in Judea' (Matthew 2:1).

The 'fixer'?

Although these prophecies point strongly to Jesus, they are not enough to *prove* that he was the Messiah. If these were the only criteria, other men might also have qualified — as critics are quick to point out. A school student once interrupted me by saying, 'But Jesus was a very smart man, and when he realized that he had been born at Bethlehem and in a family descended from David, he decided to fulfil the other prophecies too.' That brought smiles of approval from the other students, until I pointed out that as well as the prophecies about his family tree and place of birth, there were about 300 others that would have to be 'arranged' before we could condemn Jesus as a fraudulent 'fixer'.

To begin with, there are prophecies about his position or 'office'. The Old Testament said that the Messiah would be a *prophet*: 'I will raise up for them a prophet ... he will tell them everything I command him' (Deuteronomy 18:18); and in the New Testament people said of Jesus, 'A great prophet has appeared among us' (Luke 7:16). The Old Testament said that the Messiah would be 'a *priest* for ever, in the order of Melchizedek' (Psalm 110:4); and in the New Testament the quotation is applied word for word to Jesus in Hebrews 5:6. The Old Testament said that the Messiah would be a *king*: 'I have installed my king on Zion, my holy hill' (Psalm 2:6); and in the New Testament, Jesus told Pilate, 'You are right in saying I am a king' (John 18:37). The Old Testament also sees the Messiah as God's *servant*: 'Here is my servant, whom I uphold, my chosen one in whom I delight' (Isaiah 42:1); and the New Testament applies these words to Jesus in Matthew 12:18 and elsewhere.

There are also many prophecies about the amazing things the Messiah would do. Here is an excerpt from one of the most comprehensive:

'Then will the eyes of the blind be opened
    and the ears of the deaf unstopped.
Then will the lame leap like a deer,
    and the mute tongue shout for joy'

(Isaiah 35:5).

The New Testament frequently records Jesus as healing the blind, the deaf, the lame and the dumb. At one point, as a kind of interim summary, Matthew says that 'Jesus went through all the towns and villages, teaching in their synagogues, preaching the good news of the kingdom and healing every disease and sickness' (Matthew 9:35), while in ending his report John goes even further and says, 'Jesus did many other things as well. If every one of them were written down, I suppose that even the whole world would not have room for the books that would be written' (John 21:25). Could a 'fixer' simply decide to go out

and do all these things, especially when we remember that on
three separate occasions Jesus raised people from the dead?
Do you know of many people offering that kind of service in
Yellow Pages?

The last hours

But we have still not touched on one of the most significant
areas of Old Testament prophecy and New Testament fulfilment, and that is the suffering which the Messiah would endure.
No fewer than twenty-nine of these prophecies were fulfilled by
Jesus in the twenty-four hours leading up to his death. Here are
some of those predictions and their fulfilment.

- He would be forsaken by his followers: 'Strike the shepherd, and the sheep will be scattered' (Zechariah 13:7).
  When Jesus was arrested, 'everyone deserted him and
  fled' (Mark 14:50).
- He would be wrongly accused: 'Ruthless witnesses come
  forward…' (Psalm 35:11). When Jesus was on trial, 'Many
  false witnesses came forward' (Matthew 26:60).
- He would be ill treated:

> 'I offered my back to those who beat me,
>   my cheeks to those who pulled out my beard;
> I did not hide my face
>   from mocking and spitting'
> (Isaiah 50:6).

Matthew records that at one point, 'They spat in his face
and struck him with their fists. Others slapped him and said,
"Prophesy to us, Christ. Who hit you?"' (Matthew 26:67-68).

- He would not retaliate: 'He was oppressed and afflicted, yet he did not open his mouth' (Isaiah 53:7). Matthew tells us that when being bullied by Pilate, 'Jesus made no reply, not even to a single charge' (Matthew 27:14).
- He would be executed with law-breakers: 'He poured out his life unto death, and was numbered with the transgressors' (Isaiah 53:12). When Jesus was executed, 'Two robbers were crucified with him, one on his right hand and one on his left' (Matthew 27:38).
- He would be crucified (a form of execution never carried out by the Jews): 'They have pierced my hands and my feet' (Psalm 22:16). Luke records that 'When they came to the place called the Skull, there they crucified him' (Luke 23:33).
- He would pray for his executioners: 'He ... made intercession for the transgressors' (Isaiah 53:12). While hanging on the cross, Jesus prayed, 'Father, forgive them, for they do not know what they are doing' (Luke 23:34).
- None of his bones would be broken: 'The LORD ... protects all his bones, not one of them will be broken' (Psalm 34:20). Soldiers broke the legs of the two criminals to ensure their death and the removal of the bodies before the Sabbath, 'But when they came to Jesus and found that he was already dead, they did not break his legs' (John 19:33).
- His body would be pierced: 'They will look on me, the one they have pierced' (Zechariah 12:10). John's narrative goes on: 'Instead, one of the soldiers pierced Jesus' side with a spear...' (John 19:34).
- People would gamble for his clothing: 'They divide my garments among them and cast lots for my clothing' (Psalm 22:18). John says, 'When the soldiers crucified Jesus, they took his clothes, dividing them into four shares,

one for each of them, with the undergarment remaining. This garment was seamless, woven in one piece from top to bottom. "Let's not tear it," they said to one another. "Let's decide by lot who will get it"' (John 19:23-24).

What are the chances?

All that is pretty impressive — yet we have looked at only about a third of one group of twenty-nine prophecies out of a total of over 300, all of which were fulfilled to the letter in the life and death of this one man. Any talk of a 'fixer' now has a rather hollow ring about it — and becomes frankly ridiculous when we apply the law of mathematics to the case.

As I am writing this chapter, newspapers are carrying the story of a married couple who have just won an overseas holiday in a raffle held at a travel fair. As there were 799 other tickets in the draw, the odds against them doing so were 800 to one. There is nothing newsworthy about that, but the story got the media's attention because the same couple had now won the same raffle *three years running* and the odds against that were calculated at 50,000,000 to one!

Those odds are breathtaking — yet they pale into insignificance compared to the odds against Jesus fulfilling the Old Testament's Messianic prophecies by chance.

In 1958 Dr Peter W. Stoner, Professor Emeritus of Science at America's Westmont College, wrote a book entitled *Science Speaks*. In a section called 'The Christ of Prophecy', he evaluates the biblical evidence using scientific principles of probability. The American Scientific Affiliation judged his work to be 'thoroughly sound' and his application of the principles to have been done 'in a proper and convincing way'.[1] At one point he calculates the chance of just forty-eight of the Messianic prophecies being fulfilled in one person by chance at one in 10^{157}. To illustrate what this means he uses an electron, something so small that at the rate of 250 a minute, it would take 190,000,000 years to count a line of them one inch long. At the same rate, a cubic inch of electrons would take 190,000,000 x 190,000,000 x 190,000,000 years to count. Professor Stoner says that if we took this number of electrons, marked one of them, stirred them all together, then blindfolded a man and asked him to find the one we had marked, his chance of doing so would be the same as that of one man fulfilling even forty-eight of the 300 Messianic prophecies. His conclusion is that to reject the Bible's claims that Jesus is the Messiah is to reject a fact 'proved perhaps more absolutely than any other fact in the world'.[2] As he quietly refers to the quantity of electrons used in his illustrations as 'a large number'[3] we can hardly accuse him of being given to exaggeration!

The special title

The evidence that Jesus was the promised Messiah is over-whelmingly powerful — and includes the fact that in the New Testament he is identified as 'Christ' about 600 times — but he has another biblical title which takes our search for 'the real Jesus' a further important step forward: that title is *the Son of God*. The title 'son of God' is employed in several ways in the Bible. It is used of angels — spiritual beings created by God to be his worshippers, messengers and servants. The Old Testament tells us of occasions when 'the angels came to present themselves before the LORD' (Job 1:6; 2:1) and the word 'angels' translates the original Hebrew phrase for 'sons of God'. The main point being made here is that angels are like God in that they are spiritual beings without bodies. Yet the Bible teaches that while angels have great intelligence and power, they are not divine. (It is worth noting that the title 'sons of God' is

always in the plural when used of angels; we shall come back to
this later.)

Secondly, it is used of the first human beings who lived on
earth. Luke's account of Jesus' family tree goes back to creation,
all the way to 'Adam, the son of God' (Luke 3:38). Luke wants
to show that Jesus was genuinely part of the human race, and
calling Adam 'the son of God' was the simplest way of reminding his readers that Adam was the first human being God created.

Thirdly, it is used of the people of Israel as a whole. When
the Israelites were in slavery in Egypt, God told Moses to go to
Pharaoh, the Egyptian ruler, with these instructions: 'This is what
the LORD says: Israel is my firstborn son, and I told you, "Let
my son go, so that he may worship me"' (Exodus 4:22). The
picture here is of God 'adopting' Israel and going out of his
way to take special care of its people. Years later the Israelites
were reminded of this when Moses told them, 'You are the children of the LORD your God' (Deuteronomy 14:1). Later still,
when they had rebelled against God, he tenderly reminded
them: 'When Israel was a child, I loved him, and out of Egypt I
called my son' (Hosea 11:1). On another occasion God called
Ephraim, one of the twelve tribes of Israel 'my dear son' (Jeremiah 31:20), but as with the angels and Israel the reference is
to whole groups and not to individuals.

However, there is an even more important use of the title in
the Old Testament. At one point in Israel's history, God told the
prophet Nathan to take a message to King David. In it he not
only promised great security and prosperity for the nation, but
said that after David's death he would be succeeded by a great
king who would build a temple to God's glory at Jerusalem. Of
this great king God said, 'I will be his father, and he shall be my
son' (2 Samuel 7:14). This prophecy was partly fulfilled by
David's son Solomon, who completed the building of a mag-
nificent temple in 1004 B.C., but there is more to the prophecy
than meets the eye, because when two of the psalmists, David

and Ethan, referred to it later, they linked God's promise of this
coming king with the greater promise of the coming Messiah.
David applied Nathan's words to a ruler of whom God said,
'I will make the nations your inheritance, the ends of the earth
your possession' (Psalm 2:8), and even allowing for Solomon's
amazing wealth and influence, these promises cannot apply to
him. In Ethan's psalm, God referred to 'David my servant' and
added,

'I will also appoint him my firstborn,
    the most exalted of the kings of the earth.
I will maintain my love to him for ever,
    and my covenant with him will never fail.
I will establish his line for ever,
    his throne as long as the heavens endure'
(Psalm 89:27-29).

Again, not even the great king David matched up to all of this.
In other words, these psalms and the promise in 2 Samuel 7 all
had a double-barrelled meaning; they certainly referred to
earthly kings, but also to God's promise of the coming Messiah.
    We should expect to find the New Testament linking these
references with Jesus — and we do. Members of the early church
quoted Psalm 2 in one of their prayers, and connected it with
'your holy servant Jesus' (Acts 4:27). The writer of Hebrews
quoted the phrase, 'You are my Son', from the same psalm and
made it clear that God was referring to Jesus (Hebrews 5:5).
He also highlighted the significance of something we noted
earlier — that when angels were called 'sons of God' it was
always in a more general, corporate sense: 'For to which of the
angels did God ever say, "You are my Son..."?' (Hebrews 1:5).
When Paul was preaching in Pisidian Antioch he also quoted
from Psalm 2 and showed that the words 'You are my Son'
referred to Jesus (Acts 13:33). Later, in writing to the Colossians,

he took up the key word from Psalm 89 and called Jesus God's 'firstborn' (Colossians 1:18).

But these cross-references from the Old Testament are just the beginning, because the term 'Son of God' is used nearly fifty times in the New Testament, and with the exception of the reference to Adam which we noted earlier, *every one of them is used about Jesus.* Here is some of the evidence, in chronological order. Well before Jesus was born, an angel appeared to his mother Mary and told her that she would give birth to a son. She was to name him Jesus, and was told, 'He will be great and will be called the Son of the Most High' (Luke 1:32). The angel then quoted Psalm 89 (which confirms the link with the prophecies we noted) and emphasized that 'the holy one to be born will be called the Son of God' (Luke 1:35).

When Jesus was baptized (he was about thirty years old at the time) God spoke from heaven and said, 'This is my Son, whom I love; with him I am well pleased' (Matthew 3:17). This made an indelible impression on John the Baptist, who said, 'I have seen and I testify that this is the Son of God' (John 1:34). Soon after this Jesus spent forty days alone in the desert, and was then attacked by Satan. Two assaults were introduced with the words: 'If you are the Son of God...' (Matthew 4:3,6). Satan had no doubt about Jesus' identity; he was banking on it as the basis for his temptations. What he means was *'Since you are the Son of God...'* The obvious implication is that the devil had heard God's statement at Jesus' baptism — and knew that it was true. Evil spirits had the same kind of supernatural knowledge; at one point we are told that whenever they saw Jesus 'they fell down before him and cried out, "You are the Son of God"' (Mark 3:11).

Sometimes it was his power that convinced people of his identity. When Jesus stilled a storm on the Sea of Galilee, those who were there cried out, 'Truly you are the Son of God' (Matthew 14:33). When Jesus asked his disciples who they thought he was, and Simon Peter answered, 'You are the Christ, the Son of the living God' (notice the link between the Messiah and the Son of God), Jesus told him that such truth could have been revealed to him only 'by my Father in heaven' — that is, by God (Matthew 16:16-17). Peter could not have had greater confirmation than that! On another occasion God repeated the declaration he made at Jesus' baptism: 'This is my Son, whom I love; with him I am well pleased' (Matthew 17:5). All of this accumulated testimony was endorsed by the New Testament writers. Mark called his account of the life of Jesus 'the gospel about Jesus Christ, the Son of God' (Mark 1:1), while John's purpose in writing was that his readers might believe 'that Jesus is the Christ, the Son of God...' (John 20:31). Notice the significance of these two statements: as far as Mark and John were concerned they were fundamental. Other New Testament writers are equally insistent. Paul says nearly twenty times that Jesus is the Son of God, and the writer to the Hebrews does so over a dozen times.

Claims to the name

But did Jesus himself actually *claim* to be the Son of God? Again, the evidence is overwhelming. Firstly, he never once denied the title when other people gave it to him — which he certainly would have done if they had been mistaken. But there is much stronger proof than an argument from silence, and it is all the more convincing because he gave it when his life was on the line.

When Jesus was arrested and brought before the Sanhedrin, the Jews' top political and religious tribunal, Caiaphas the high priest asked him the straightforward question: 'Tell us if you are the Christ, the Son of God.' Without any hesitation or evasion, Jesus replied, 'Yes, it is as you say' (Matthew 26:63-64). That sounds conclusive enough, but his answer becomes even more impressive when we notice that Jesus was charged to answer 'under oath by the living God'. Of all the oaths in Jewish law, this was by far the most serious. Anyone charged under it was obliged to answer, and holding back part of the truth or obscuring it in any way would be unthinkable. In the face of that kind of pressure, the answer Jesus gave was incapable of being misunderstood, and produced a verdict of blasphemy from Caiaphas and a beating-up by his accusers.

The next day Jesus was hauled before the Sanhedrin again, but no amount of 'softening-up' could make him change his mind. When asked, 'Are you then the Son of God?' he replied, 'You are right in saying I am' (Luke 22:70). The authorities were furious, and wanted to kill him there and then, but under the rules of the Roman occupation of the country they had no right to execute anyone, but had to refer the case to Pontius Pilate, the Roman governor. Pilate brushed aside the vague charge that Jesus was 'a criminal' (John 18:30), but ordered Jesus to be flogged, hoping that that would satisfy them. But the Jews were after blood, and when Pilate insisted, 'I find no basis for a charge against him' (John 19:6) they played their trump card: 'We have a law, and according to that law he must die, because he claimed to be the Son of God' (John 19:7). At any point in all of this Jesus could have saved his skin by withdrawing that claim or by saying that he meant to say only that as a Jew he was part of a nation which God had called 'my son'. Instead, he allowed himself to be stripped, beaten, mocked, flogged and crucified — and never retracted a word.

The unique relationship

But what did Jesus mean by claiming to be the Son of God? We usually think of a 'son' in terms of relationship, but Scripture shows that this particular relationship was unique in several ways.

Firstly, it was a *special* relationship. When his disciples asked how they should pray, Jesus taught them what we now call 'the Lord's Prayer'. This began with the words, 'Our Father in heaven...' (Matthew 6:9), which he encouraged them to use as devout believers who trusted in God. Yet we are never told that he joined them in using this phrase. Surely that tells us something? If 'Our Father' was the right way to address God, why not join his disciples in doing so? Jesus refers to God as 'Father' about 170 times, yet not once does he use the pronoun 'our' to link himself with others. Instead, he went out of his way to show that his relationship with God was totally different from that of anyone else; he spoke of the time when he would return 'to my Father and your Father, to my God and your God' (John 20:17). That statement is either arrogant or significant!

Secondly, it was an *intimate* relationship. This comes across very powerfully in a remarkable passage in which we 'overhear' Jesus at prayer just before his arrest. He began, 'Abba, Father...' (Mark 14:36). The word 'Abba' is Aramaic (the language Jesus spoke) and the significant thing about it is that it is a very familiar and informal word. Some even say that it was the word a little child might use of its earthly father — something like our English word 'Daddy' — but that might be carrying it too far. What we do know is that *nobody before him in all the Bible's history had ever addressed God in this way*. Devout Jews were used to the idea of calling God 'Father' but *never*, under any circumstances, would they have addressed him as 'Abba'. Yet Jesus did — naturally, deliberately and knowingly. There can surely be only one explanation: he knew that his relationship with God was deeper and more intimate than that which any other human being had ever experienced.

Thirdly, it was an *eternal* relationship. Some people have suggested that Jesus was just an ordinary man who 'became' the Son of God at some time in his life as a kind of reward for his obedience, faithfulness or holiness. This would mean that although he was better than other men, he was not essentially *different*. But as soon as we examine the evidence, this theory disintegrates. During a visit to the temple at Jerusalem when he was just twelve years old, he spoke of being 'in my Father's house' (Luke 2:49) — nearly twenty years before his public ministry began. Nor is it good enough to suggest that Jesus 'became' the Son of God at his birth, because the Bible says otherwise. For example, at one point he prays, 'And now, Father, glorify me in your presence with the glory I had with you *before the world began*' (John 17:5). Those words are saying that in some way Jesus shared God the Father's glory with him before even the world existed! Other New Testament writers reinforce them. Paul writes about God 'sending his own Son...' (Romans 8:3). (Notice that Jesus is said to be God's Son before he was sent.) He tells the Galatians that at exactly the right moment in history 'God sent his Son, born of a woman...' (Galatians 4:4). (Notice that Jesus is said to have been God's 'Son' before he was 'born'!) The apostle John says that God 'sent his one and only Son into the world' (1 John 4:9).

This is getting us into very deep water. What we are being told is that Jesus of Nazareth (who was, as we saw in an earlier chapter, as human as we are) was the Son of God before he was born, even before the world came into being, and shared God the Father's glory within a unique, intimate and *eternal* relationship. That points to something infinitely greater than anything we have unearthed thus far in our investigation — and we will find out what that is later on. For the time being we need to step back and discover what happened when Jesus was born.

4.

The man with no beginning

Biographies essentially begin with the birth of the person concerned. The writer may say something about the social or political conditions at the time, or about the subject's family background, but all of this is preliminary to the point at which the story really begins. Yet the birth is dealt with very quickly. After all, one person's entry into the world is very much like another's: conception, gestation, contractions, labour, delivery — and the reason biographers skip over it in a line or two is that the product of all this activity makes no conscious contribution to any of it!

But in the birth of Jesus we come up against a factor which makes him unique in human culture. Not to beat about the bush, the Bible says that when Jesus was born his mother was a virgin. This is usually referred to as the 'Virgin Birth', but that is rather misleading, because there is no evidence of anything unusual about the birth of Jesus. As far as we know he left his mother's womb in the usual way. What is unique is not how Jesus *left* his mother's womb, but how he *entered* it, and on this the Bible is clear. There are no small print, no 'ifs' or 'buts'. What it says is that Jesus was conceived in his mother's womb without sexual intercourse, without any injection of male sperm, without any rupture of the hymen. In medical terms, his mother became pregnant while still *virgo intacta*.

Who believes in miracles?

I fully appreciate that that last paragraph will be enough to switch some people off. A woman having a baby without receiving male sperm? Ridiculous! That would take a miracle — and miracles do not happen! That sounds pretty conclusive — but it is not.

What is a miracle? The English word literally means 'something to be wondered at', but for the time being we can probably go along with this as a working definition: 'An event or action that apparently contradicts known scientific laws.'[1] For some people, that says it all. Anything that contradicts the scientific laws governing our world of time and space (which is assumed to be operating within its own closed mechanism) is not only suspect but can safely be rejected. That argument used to be paraded around with great assurance, but it is pretty old hat now, especially since Einstein's theory of relativity opened up man's understanding of the universe.

In 1969 Professor Sir Norman Anderson wrote a book called *Christianity: the witness of history* and included a lengthy section on miracles. By the time the second edition of the book was published in 1985, under the revised title of *Jesus Christ: the witness of history*, this section was reduced to a few lines. His main reason for doing so was 'because the one-time insistence of scientists on the uniformity of nature and her "laws" is today much less obtrusive; for physicists, doctors and others have come increasingly to realize that the exceptional and unexpected does happen from time to time and that cause and effect do not invariably follow the normal pattern'.

In other words, rejecting the possibility of miracles on purely scientific grounds is unscientific! In 1984 the Bishop of Durham caused a rumpus by casting doubt on the virgin conception of Jesus (bishops, after all, are meant to support biblical doctrine, not sabotage it). As a result, fourteen prominent scientists, most of them university professors, wrote a letter to *The Times*. Their spokesman was the geneticist Professor R. J. Berry, President of the Linnean Society, and the letter included the following statement: 'It is not logically valid to use science as an argument against miracles. To believe that miracles cannot happen is as much an act of faith as to believe that they can happen. Miracles are unprecedented events. Whatever the current fashions in philosophy or the revelations of opinion polls may suggest, it is important to affirm that science (based as it is on the observation of precedents) *can have nothing to say on the subject*.'[2] The italics are mine; the conclusion is theirs, and anyone anxious to obliterate the miraculous must reckon with it. They must also reckon with the statement by Blaise Pascal, the seventeenth-century French genius who was philosopher, physicist, mathematician and theologian rolled into one (to say nothing of being the inventor of the calculator), that 'it is impossible on reasonable grounds to destroy miracles'.

The philosophical argument against miracles also makes discussion pointless because it begins from the same premise — that miracles *cannot* happen. As C. S. Lewis says, 'Those who assume that miracles cannot happen are merely wasting their time by looking into the texts: we know in advance what results they will find, for they have begun by begging the question.'[3]

In other words, the problem is not the reliability of the evidence, but the presuppositions that people bring to the case, and the greatest of these is the one that denies the existence of God. The modern scholar Dr Henry Morris writes, 'To say that miracles are impossible is to deny that God exists.'[4] This may be going a little too far (people could believe in God but not believe that he would 'interfere' with his creation) but it points us in the right direction: *we cannot believe in the God of the Bible and rule out the miraculous*. As Robert Horn puts it, 'A non-supernatural God is a contradiction in terms. If God exists at all, *he is God* — with powers, wisdom and knowledge infinitely greater than ours.'[5] Later on, with specific reference to the virgin conception of Jesus, he adds this: 'If I say this is impossible, I'm claiming more than I dare. I, who am frail, finite, fallible, failed — how can I pronounce on what is feasible to God? The supernatural is God's lifestyle, his business, his *métier*, his decision.' That is a rather elegant way of saying what could be put much more bluntly: to deny that God performs miracles is to display both ignorance and arrogance. In fact, it will be helpful if we think of a miracle as 'an event brought about by the immediate agency of God in contrast with his ordinary method of working'.[6]

It may be worth mentioning that in neither of the Bible's basic languages (Hebrew and Greek) is there a word which exactly corresponds to our concept of 'miracle'. Instead, there are words which we can properly translate 'wonders' (things which excite attention and awe), 'signs' (extraordinary and purposeful acts of God), and 'powers' (which demand more than the power of man). The word 'miracle' is one we have invented to cover these concepts.

As soon as we bring God into the reckoning, the whole picture changes. Since God framed the laws which govern the universe, surely he has the right to bring other laws into operation whenever he chooses? The American theologian J. Gresham Machen links this with God's power in creation: 'What God has done once, he can obviously do again. He acted independently of nature when he created the course of nature in the first place. He may, therefore, act in equal independence of the course of nature at any time he will.'[7] The apostle Paul took exactly the same kind of line when he was defending traditional Old Testament doctrine before the pagan King Agrippa and others: 'Why should any of you consider it incredible that *God* raises the dead?' (Acts 26:8). (The italics are mine, but I suspect that Paul gave the word the same emphasis!) Once we accept the independent, supernatural power of God, there is no scientific, philosophical or logical reason for refusing to accept any of his actions. God is not in a rut, unable to do anything new or different. However spectacular they appear to us, miracles are no problem to God. Nor is even the greatest miracle the slightest interruption of events as far as God is concerned. In God's mind there is no distinction between the 'natural' and the 'supernatural'. Everything God does is consistent not only with his own perfection but with his wise, loving and eternal purposes.

Ultimately the question is not 'Can miracles happen?' but 'Have they happened?', and each case must be examined in the light of the evidence. Let us return to the case in hand.

The facts

The narratives of the birth of Jesus come to us from the pens of two New Testament writers, Matthew and Luke, both men whose occupations called for accuracy of expression and attention to detail. Matthew was a civil servant, working in one of the local taxation departments, and although many ancient tax collectors were notorious 'fiddlers', there is no evidence that taints Matthew in this way. Luke was a doctor, and his writing underlines his attention to detail. While Mark speaks of a man with 'a shrivelled hand' (Mark 3:1), Luke says that the man's 'right hand was shrivelled' (Luke 6:6). Matthew says that Peter's mother-in-law had 'a fever' (Matthew 8:14); Luke says that she was 'suffering from a *high fever*' (Luke 4:38), using exactly the right medical word to identify serious conditions of this kind. This attention to detail ought to tell us that of all people he would be the least likely to invent a story which would contradict all his medical knowledge and make him the laughing-stock of his fellow GPs.

Now to the narratives themselves. Here is Matthew's account: 'This is how the birth of Jesus Christ came about: His mother Mary was pledged to be married to Joseph, but before they came together, she was found to be with child through the Holy Spirit. Because Joseph her husband was a righteous man and did not want to expose her to public disgrace, he had in mind to divorce her quietly. But after he had considered this, an angel of the Lord appeared to him in a dream and said, "Joseph, son of David, do not be afraid to take Mary home as your wife, because what is conceived in her is from the Holy Spirit. She will give birth to a son, and you are to give him the name Jesus, because he will save his people from their sins"' (Matthew 1:18-21). A little later, Matthew ends his narrative like this: 'When Joseph woke up, he did what the angel of the Lord had commanded him and took Mary home as his wife. But he had no union with her until she gave birth to a son. And he gave him the name Jesus' (Matthew 1:24-25).

Notice that Matthew's account begins with Mary 'pledged to be married to Joseph'. This was the second of three stages in traditional Jewish marriage procedure. The first was called an engagement, and sometimes took place when the two people concerned were still children. Their fathers might agree on the match, or a kind of matrimonial agency might suggest it. It was more of an arrangement than an engagement as we know it today. The second stage was the betrothal, when the man and woman concerned 'pledged' themselves to each other. This was a solemn and binding step, taken in the presence of witnesses. Though continuing to live separately, from that moment on they would be called 'husband' and 'wife' (Matthew uses those very words). This step was so serious that they could not be separated except by divorce, and any infidelity was regarded as adultery. If one of them died while pledged, the survivor was treated as a widow or widower. This stage of being pledged lasted for about a year, and led finally to the *marriage* when they set up home together.

As Matthew makes clear, it was during the second of these three stages that they discovered that Mary was pregnant. At this point the cynic might say, 'So what? They had an "accident"', but Matthew scotches that idea by confirming that the pregnancy began 'before they came together'. Joseph was stunned. He knew he was not responsible, and while he could hardly bring himself to believe that Mary had been sleeping around, that seemed to be the only explanation. The one thing he did know was that the marriage was off. To legalize their separation, he would have to divorce her, using one of two options open to him under Jewish law. He could drag her before a magistrate and force her to confess her unfaithfulness and immorality, or he could sign the necessary papers privately in the presence of two witnesses. Out of consideration for Mary he took the second course, and decided to 'divorce her quietly'. But before he could do this, an angel appeared to Joseph in a dream and told him that he could safely take Mary home as his wife because her pregnancy was not the result of any sin on her part but of a miraculous act by the Holy Spirit. What is more, Mary would carry the baby to term, she would give birth to a son, and he was to be given the name Jesus 'because he will save his people from their sins'.

Matthew then tells us that Joseph did exactly as he was told and that the marriage went ahead, but he adds one significant detail: Joseph 'had no union with her until she gave birth to a son'. There was no reason why they should not have had intercourse immediately after marriage (as they obviously had later because we are told in Mark 6:3 that Jesus had brothers and sisters), but Matthew's account ends with a specific statement of Mary's virginity prior to the birth of Jesus.

The doctor's report

In Luke's account the story is reported from Mary's viewpoint. This is how it reads: 'In the sixth month, God sent the angel Gabriel to Nazareth, a town in Galilee, to a virgin pledged to be married to a man name Joseph, a descendant of David. The virgin's name was Mary. The angel went to her and said, "Greetings, you who are highly favoured! The Lord is with you." Mary was greatly troubled at his words and wondered what kind of greeting this might be. But the angel said to her, "Do not be afraid, Mary, you have found favour with God. You will be with child and give birth to a son, and you are to give him the name Jesus. He will be great and will be called the Son of the Most High. The Lord God will give him the throne of his father David, and he will reign over the house of Jacob for ever; his kingdom will never end." "How will this be," Mary asked the angel, "since I am a virgin?" The angel answered, "The Holy Spirit will come upon you, and the power of the Most High will overshadow you. So the holy one to be born will be called the Son of God. Even Elizabeth your relative is going to have a child in her old age, and she who was said to be barren is in her sixth month. For nothing is impossible with God." "I am the Lord's servant," Mary answered. "May it be to me as you have said." Then the angel left her' (Luke 1:26-38).

Let us examine the doctor's report in detail. It begins a little earlier than Matthew's, because Mary was not yet pregnant when the angel appeared to her. His first words were to assure her that there was nothing to fear; she had found favour with God. Mary was speechless. No doubt she was shocked by the appearance of an angel (which is hardly an everyday occurrence!) but Luke says that she was 'greatly troubled at his words'. Then the angel came to the point. She would find herself pregnant and give birth to a son, who was to be given the name Jesus. Although there was nothing unusual in a young woman becoming pregnant, it was amazing to have the child's sex established over nine months before its birth, and remarkable to be given instructions from God about the child's name. Yet they still left Mary with a fundamental problem: 'How will this be, since I am a virgin?' She did not seem to question the promises, but was totally baffled as to how these things would come about. Mary knew the facts of life: before there could be a birth there would have to be conception, and before conception, intercourse — and she was a virgin. Then how could these things happen?

The angel's reply tied in exactly with the message given to Joseph. In the power of the Holy Spirit, God would work a biological miracle in her womb and bring about a virgin conception, which would lead to the birth of a baby boy who would not be the son of her husband Joseph but in a unique way the Son of God. The angel went on to remind her of a miracle that had happened to one of her relatives. Elizabeth and her husband Zechariah 'had no children, because Elizabeth was barren; and they were both well on in years' (Luke 1:7), yet now Elizabeth was six months pregnant, because 'nothing is impossible with God'. With a beautiful blend of simplicity, humility and obedience Mary replied, 'I am the Lord's servant. May it be to me as you have said.'

The doctor's ante-natal report ends there. It is crisp, concise and clear; and three times it confirms that Mary was a virgin when Jesus was conceived. Not only that, but later Luke calls Jesus 'the son, *so it was thought*, of Joseph' (Luke 3:23), showing that at that stage public opinion was at odds with the facts.

Critics' corner

Not surprisingly, the virgin conception of Jesus has been strongly challenged. One suggestion is that the Jews were rather puritanical about sexual matters and considered intercourse to be in some way 'unclean', and as this would not seem an appropriate beginning for someone called the Son of God, they invented the idea of a virgin conception. But this is a feeble argument, because elsewhere in the New Testament sexuality is treated with healthy normality. As Professor Alan Richardson says, 'This morbid notion of sexuality is totally absent from the Jewish mind in general and from the birth records of the Gospels in particular.'[8]

Other critics have suggested that the New Testament narratives were invented by the followers of Jesus to match or outdo stories surrounding the births of pagan gods, religious leaders or kings. Buddha's mother claimed that a white elephant with six tusks 'entered my belly'.[9] The mother of Perseus, one of the gods of Greek mythology, was said to have been impregnated by a shower of golden rain containing Zeus, the king of the gods. Alexander the Great was alleged to have had an even more exotic genesis: his mother Olympias cheated on her husband, Philip of Macedon, by sleeping with Zeus, who had turned himself into a serpent for the occasion! But the simplicity and purity of the New Testament narrative bears no likeness to these absurd and obscene fairy tales; in one scholar's words, it is 'bathed in holiness'.[10] The idea that the Gospels are aping the gods is frankly nonsensical, and there is not a shred of evidence that the New Testament writers even knew of those ridiculous myths.

Inevitably there have been 'natural' and 'scientific' objections to the supernatural conception of Jesus. For example, the liberal theologian Henry Emerson Fosdick said that the birth of Jesus was recorded 'in terms of a biological miracle that our modern minds cannot use';[11] but we have already shown that to dispose of miracles by saying that they cannot happen is philosophically and scientifically dishonest. Some people have tried to compromise by suggesting that what we have here is a startling case of parthenogenesis — the female egg dividing itself without any male fertilization. This kind of thing has been observed in some lower mammal forms, though according to a study carried out at Cambridge University some years ago no viable young developed as a result. But this theory comes unstuck for a much more basic reason. In the genetic make-up of human beings, the male has x and y chromosomes, while the female has x and x. This means that if Mary's pregnancy had been triggered off by some biological freak (even if it was the only one in history) the child born as a result would have been *female*, because no y chromosome would have been present to produce a male child.

Others have doubted the virgin conception of Jesus because there is no other explicit reference to it in the New Testament, but the argument from silence is notoriously unreliable. As Dr A. Rendle Short once wrote, 'Shakespeare never mentions Canterbury, St. Paul's, Winchester or Durham cathedrals; shall we conclude that he never heard of them?'[12] Silence is hardly the same as denial! One could also add that there are some very strong hints that the apostle Paul (who wrote more of the New Testament than anyone else) believed it to be true. He says that 'God sent his Son, *born of a woman*' (Galatians 4:4). The phrase *might* mean no more than that Jesus was a genuine human being — Job calls men in general 'born of woman' (Job 14:1) and Jesus said that John the Baptist was outstanding among 'those born of women' (Matthew 11:11) — but it is an unusual phrase, and one which might well hint at the idea of a virgin conception. The great theologian John Calvin went so far as to say that in context the phrase 'was expressly intended to distinguish Christ from other men, as having been formed of the substance of his mother and not by ordinary generation'.[13]

Paul also says that Adam was a 'pattern of the one to come' (Romans 5:14). The meaning is that Adam was a kind of proto-type of Jesus, and part of Paul's argument at this point is that just as Adam was the starting-point of the human race, so Jesus marked a totally new beginning and was the starting-point of a new humanity. This may not specifically endorse the virgin conception of Jesus, but the link with Adam (who for other and obvious reasons did not have a human father) fits perfectly into the picture. As Thomas Boston wrote, 'Christ was an extraordinary person, and another Adam; and therefore it was necessary he should be produced a new way. At first, Adam was produced neither of man nor woman; Eve of man without a woman; all others of a man and a woman. The fourth way remained, viz. of a woman without a man; and so Christ was born.'[14]

Writing to the Corinthians, Paul makes the link even more explicit, and refers to Adam as 'the first man' and to Jesus as 'the second man', to Adam as 'the earthly man' and to Jesus as 'the man from heaven' (1 Corinthians 15:47-48). Again, while there is no specific mention of the virgin birth, it is a fact, as Douglas Edwards points out, that 'St Paul, without a word of explanation, can speak of Christ as "the second man". It is as though there had been something in the nature of a fresh creation.'[15] As Edwards adds, 'The real question is how, being man, he himself got the fresh start, or again how he could be the head of a race of which (if born like others) he was but, with us, a fellow member. On the other hand if — as all the evidence goes to show — the Virgin Birth was an integral part of Christian doctrine from the first, then (for St Paul and his readers) Adam was a type of the Christ to come.'[16]

Part of the whole

The way in which the virgin conception fits into the rest of the Bible (and is never once contradicted) comes across even more impressively when we look at some of the Old Testament prophecies about the great Deliverer promised by God. Let us take just three examples. The first is where God told Satan,

'I will put enmity
  between you and the woman,
  and between your offspring and hers;
he will crush your head,
  and you will strike his heel'

(Genesis 3:15).

In this remarkable statement God says that there would be continual conflict between the devil and mankind, man would be hurt by the devil's activity ('you will strike his heel') and that the devil would eventually be overcome by someone who would be a *woman's* offspring, a phrase found nowhere else in the Old Testament. The turning-point in mankind's battle against forces of evil that were to cause him so much suffering would come through the offspring of a woman. This does seem like a very telling hint.

The second prophecy came about 700 years before Jesus was born, when through the prophet Isaiah God gave this promise to Ahaz, the eleventh King of Judah: 'Therefore the Lord himself will give you a sign: The virgin will be with child and will give birth to a son, and will call him Immanuel' (Isaiah 7:14). This particular prophecy has attracted so much attention that we need to look at it in some detail. The background is that in the reign of Ahaz, Judah was under threat from the allied forces of Syria and Israel. The prophet Isaiah assured Ahaz that the attacks would fail and that Syria and Israel would be destroyed. When Ahaz refused to ask for God's offer of a miraculous sign to confirm this prophecy, God graciously gave the nation the promise we have just noted, adding that Judah's enemies would be killed 'before the boy knows enough to reject the wrong and choose the right' (Isaiah 7:16).

This may well be one of those 'double-barrelled' prophecies fulfilled in a localized and contemporary way and then in a fuller way later on, and if this is the case there were several candidates for the role of the child's mother.

But it is not difficult to see that Isaiah's prophecy also anticipates the birth of Jesus. Some of those who deny this have pointed out that Isaiah's word for 'virgin' (the Hebrew *almah*) could mean no more than 'a young woman' and that if he had wanted to be clear about the young woman's unmarried virginity he would have used the word *bethulah*. But the argument has more weaknesses than strengths. Firstly, although the word *bethulah* can mean a virgin, another Old Testament writer uses the word of someone 'grieving for the husband of her youth' (Joel 1:8) — which means that if he had used that word Isaiah could have had in mind a married woman (and presumably not a virgin). Secondly, in the Septuagint, the first Greek translation of the Old Testament, the translators always rendered *almah* as *parthenos*, a word which can *only* mean 'virgin' — and as this translation was made in the third century we can hardly accuse them of manipulating their translation of Isaiah 7:14 to fit in with the birth of Jesus! Thirdly, while the word *almah* means no more than 'a young woman of marriageable age' it would be unnatural to use it other than of someone who was unmarried and at least by implication a virgin. This is borne out by the nine occasions in which the word occurs in the Old Testament. Not once is it clearly used of a woman who is not a virgin, and certainly never of a married woman. Martin Luther once offered 100 *gulden* to anyone who could show that *almah* ever referred to a married woman (and added that the Lord alone knew where he could get the money!). Nobody took up the challenge.

Far from the word *almah* being a weakness in linking Isaiah's prophecy to the birth of Jesus, it proves to be the opposite. The

American theologian and linguist Edward J.Young says it seems to be 'the only word in the language which unequivocally signifies an unmarried woman. No other available Hebrew word would clearly indicate that the one who it designates was unmarried. Consequently, no other word would have been suitable for fulfilling the requirements of the sign such as the context demanded. None of these other words would have pointed to an unusual birth.'[17]

Matthew certainly had no hesitation in seeing the birth of Jesus as the fulfilment of this particular prophecy. He wrote, 'All this took place to fulfil what the Lord had said through the prophet: "The virgin [*parthenos*] will be with child and will give birth to a son, and they will call him Immanuel" — which means "God with us"' (Matthew 1:22).

The third prophecy comes about 100 years after Isaiah, when God gave this promise to the people of Judah:

'How long will you wander,
    O unfaithful daughter?
The LORD will create a new thing on earth —
    a woman will surround a man'
(Jeremiah 31:22).

Again, this seems to be a double-barrelled prophecy. In the immediate context it was fulfilled when Israel (compared here to a weak young woman) overcame its powerful enemies (the 'man'). But it is not difficult to sense an even richer meaning in the words and to see how perfectly they forecast the virgin conception of Jesus. Notice these six points. Firstly, the promised event would be carried out by 'the LORD'; it would be something accomplished by God alone; and Jesus was conceived 'by the power of the Most High'. Secondly, God would create 'a new thing', something unprecedented in human history; and when Mary was 'found to be with child through the Holy Spirit', and gave birth while still a virgin, this was certainly something unique. Thirdly, this startling event would happen 'on earth', the literal meaning of which is 'in the land' (in other words, the land of Judah); and that is exactly where Jesus was born. Fourthly, a 'woman' would be involved in the birth, but there is no mention of a husband or father — the child would come not from nothing (as did Adam), nor from man (as did Eve), nor from a man and a woman (as did everyone else) but from a woman; and we are specifically told that Joseph had no sexual intercourse with Mary 'until she gave birth to a son'. Fifthly, the woman would 'surround' a man. The Hebrew word translated 'surround' is used in Genesis 2:11,13 of a river which 'winds through' (or around) a country, and in Psalm 71:21 of the writer's assurance that God would 'comfort' him in time of need. The word is therefore beautifully suited to the picture of a woman conceiving and enclosing a child within her womb. Finally this woman would surround 'a man'. The word used is not one of the three most common Hebrew words for 'man' (adam, ish, or enosi) but geber, the root meaning of which is to be strong or heroic; and the angel promised Mary that her child would be 'great'. What is more, this same word is the very one used of the Messiah 100 years after Jeremiah's prophecy, when God called him 'the man [geber] who is close to me' (Zechariah 13:7).

   If all of this is not an Old Testament prophecy of a New Testament event we have to settle for a wagonload of coincidences that makes it even more remarkable!

Questions

Determined sceptics have an endless shelf life, and there will always be those who for one reason or another try to argue away the Gospel records. Yet they will always be faced with these questions, based on the supposition that Mary was not a virgin when Jesus was conceived.

- Why did the early church invent a story which would immediately result in ridicule, scorn and contempt? Surely the best counter to the grotesque birth stories of other religions would be something acceptable to prospective recruits?
- Why did Luke, a medical expert, never deviate from his convictions despite all the pressure that surely would have been put on him?
- Why was the story not refuted by anyone within the church during the first two centuries when the first Christian creeds were being formulated? Surely someone would have suggested that they drop such an embarrassing invention from their manifesto?
- Why have contemporary records not produced even one credible alternative?
- Why has the church always treated Mary with such reverence (some people even going to the unbiblical lengths of worshipping her) if she was no more than a common or garden fornicator?
- How has the church reconciled the illegitimate conception of Jesus with its insistence that chastity before marriage is God's inflexible law?
- Surely an illegitimate conception casts aspersions on God's moral integrity, because the records tell us that Mary (who would have been dishonest and immoral) found favour with God?
- If the biblical record is not accurate, how can we trust anything written by Matthew or Luke?

All the available evidence indicates that Jesus entered the world by a unique miracle brought about by the unaided power of God for his own glory and for the good of his people. It was beautifully expressed by Matthew Henry, the well-known eighteenth-century Bible commentator. Linking the birth of Jesus with the remarkable way in which Eve, the first woman, came into the world, he wrote, 'The God who took a motherless woman out of the side of a man took a fatherless man out of the body of a woman.'[18]

We are now ready to take the next step towards uncovering 'the real Jesus'.

5.

The man who got it right

It should come as no surprise that the Bible's claims about the birth of Jesus have prompted a whole series of fantastic stories and theories about him. As far back as the first century people called Docetists taught that Jesus was a kind of phantom, whose body was not real. In the fourth century a group called Apollinarians taught that Jesus had a human anatomy but not a human psychology, a human body but not a human spirit. In modern times, Mary Baker Eddy, the founder of Christian Science, wrote, 'Christ is in incorporeal,' which in effect says that his body was not a body — which does seem to be stretching things a bit, even for an organization that is neither Christian nor scientific!

The marks of a man

But when we turn to the evidence all these hare-brained ideas are blown apart, because the Bible overwhelmingly establishes that Jesus was fully, truly and totally human.

Firstly, there is the evidence of his *physical life*. As we saw in the previous chapter, he had a perfectly normal birth. After pregnancy Mary his mother 'gave birth to her firstborn, a son' (Luke 2:7). Then we are told that when he was eight days old 'it was time to circumcise him' (Luke 2:21). Circumcision was an important practice commanded in the Old Testament as a symbol of God's covenant with his people, and Jesus was circumcised just like any other Hebrew boy.

He experienced all the normal stages of physical development — he 'grew in wisdom and stature' (Luke 2:52). He had to be taught to stand, to walk, to speak, to write, to feed and dress himself. His hair grew, his muscles expanded, his voice broke, he passed through puberty into manhood. He also showed all the usual physical limitations. He needed to be sustained by food and drink. There were times when 'he was hungry' (Matthew 21:18). When dying he called out, 'I am thirsty' (John 19:28). After a long day's travel he was 'tired … from the journey' (John 4:6). At the end of the day we find him 'sleeping' (Matthew 8:24). All of this clearly points to his real humanity. He was neither superman nor supermyth, but truly, genuinely human.

Feelings count

Secondly, there is the evidence of his *emotional life*, in which he displayed a whole range of normal human feelings. To begin with one of the most powerful of all human emotions, we read that 'Jesus loved Martha and her sister and Lazarus' (John 11:5). His relationship with certain people was expressed as friendship: he once told his followers, 'I have called you friends' (John 15:15). He knew great sadness: when his friend Lazarus died, 'Jesus wept' (John 11:35) and when he realized that the city of Jerusalem was heading for disaster, he 'wept over it' (Luke 19:41). On the other hand, he also had times of great joy. There is no record of him laughing, or even smiling, but it would surely be too much to suggest that he never did? There are marks of genuine humour in several of the stories he told, and when his disciples reported their successes to him he was 'full of joy' (Luke 10:21).

He had great sympathy for people in need. When he sensed that people were being harassed by religious rigmarole, 'he had compassion on them' (Matthew 9:36). When he came across a deaf mute he expressed his feelings 'with a deep sigh' (Mark 7:34). We can be sure that in the course of thirty or so years he ran through a whole gamut of emotional trauma. We get a glimpse of this as he approached his death: he 'began to be deeply distressed and troubled' and told his disciples, 'My soul is overwhelmed with sorrow' (Mark 14:33-34). The words blend a wide range of emotions, including shock, fear, confusion, distress, agitation, mental agony, spiritual pain, despondency and horror. If ever his humanity showed through it was in those terrible hours.

Body and soul

Thirdly, we see the humanity of Jesus in his *spiritual life*. The most obvious thing to notice is that he prayed. We are specifically told of some twenty-five instances, and Luke says that 'Jesus often withdrew to lonely places and prayed' (Luke 5:16). He regularly attended public worship; Luke tells of an occasion when 'on the Sabbath day he went into the synagogue, *as was his custom*' (Luke 4:16). He read his Bible; we know this because he was constantly quoting Scripture, almost always from memory, and often challenged his critics with phrases like 'Have you never read in the Scriptures...?' (Matthew 21:42).

Finally he was tempted. He went through one particularly horrendous time alone in the desert, 'where for forty days he was tempted by the devil' (Luke 4:2), but this was not his only experience of temptation because when it was over the devil only left him 'until an opportune time' (Luke 4:13). But the clearest statement about this comes later in the New Testament when we read that he was 'tempted in every way, just as we are' (Hebrews 4:15). He knew the pain and pressure of fighting against sin, the struggle to live a godly life in a godless world, the agony of spiritual conflict. But here, too, he was unique, because the same sentence that says he was 'tempted in every way, just as we are' adds the amazing words: '*yet was without sin*'. Once again we are faced with a statement that sets Jesus apart from everyone else in history, and the evidence to back it up comes from at least five unusual and impressive sources.

The opposition

The first indication we have of the sinlessness of Jesus is that *his enemies admitted it* — though of course not all of them. During his public ministry Jesus was accused of all kinds of things, but these accusations were so ridiculous that one hardly knows whether to laugh or cry when reading them. For example, when he accepted an invitation to the home of a reformed swindler, people muttered, 'He has gone to be the guest of a "sinner"' (Luke 19:7) — as if that were a crime! When some shady characters gathered around to listen to him, the religious leaders complained, 'This man welcomes sinners' (Luke 15:2) — as if a religious teacher should never do such a thing! When he healed a man with a withered hand the Pharisees accused him of breaking the law by doing so on the Sabbath, and 'began to plot with the Herodians how they might kill Jesus' (Mark 3:6). On other occasions they accused him of being a glutton, a drunkard, demon-possessed and a traitor — all without a single shred of evidence.

Much more impressive is the testimony to his *innocence* given in the final hours before his death. Despite heavy pressure by the religious authorities (who had hauled Jesus before them on

yet another trumped-up charge) the Roman governor Pontius
Pilate had to admit, 'I find no basis for a charge against him'
(John 18:38). While the trial was still in progress, Pilate's wife
warned him, 'Don't have anything to do with that innocent
man, for I have suffered a great deal today in a dream because
of him' (Matthew 27:19). No details of the dream are given,
nor is there any explanation, but perhaps Pilate had discussed
the case with his wife, and the possibility of an innocent man
being executed had been preying on her mind.

Then we have the confession of Judas Iscariot, who had
accepted a bribe to betray Jesus to the authorities. When Jesus
was eventually condemned to death Judas was suddenly 'seized
with remorse and returned the thirty silver coins to the chief
priests and the elders. "I have sinned," he said, "for I have
betrayed innocent blood"' (Matthew 27:3-4). That is a more
powerful testimony than Pilate's, because Judas had been with
Jesus for three years and had every opportunity to judge his
character. Now his conscience gripped him like a vice, and when
the authorities turned a deaf ear to him he went out and hanged
himself.

Next comes the statement by one of the two criminals executed alongside Jesus. At one stage, both of them hurled insults
at him. Then one of them changed tack. Perhaps remembering
some of the things that had been said about Jesus, he cried,
'Aren't you the Christ? Save yourself and us!' (Luke 23:39). His
partner protested: '"Don't you fear God," he said, "since you
are under the same sentence? We are punished justly, for we
are getting what our deeds deserve. But this man has done
nothing wrong"' (Luke 23:40-41). The particular phrase he used
means something like 'He never put a foot wrong.' Whatever
the man's basis for saying this, it remains an unusual and surprising piece of evidence.

Finally there is a statement by the Roman army officer in
charge of the execution squad. When Jesus finally breathed his

last, this hardened professional soldier, no doubt familiar with
the behaviour of criminals facing death, cried out, 'Surely this
was a righteous man' (Luke 23:47). The word 'righteous' means
much more than 'good'. It means 'upright in the sight of God',
and makes the soldier's testimony even more striking.

Those who changed their minds

Not only did his enemies indicate the innocence of Jesus, but
his followers believed it. The best example is the apostle Paul.
Originally called Saul of Tarsus, he developed into a strictly
orthodox Pharisee, conscientious in his observance of Hebrew
ceremonial laws and an avid student of the Old Testament. He
was so bitterly opposed to Jesus and his followers that he began
a personal crusade to destroy the early Christians. At one stage
we find him 'breathing out murderous threats against the Lord's
disciples' and getting official permission to arrest them and 'take
them as prisoners to Jerusalem' (Acts 9:1-2).

But something happened to Saul, something that brought
about a complete transformation in this brilliant, highly edu-
cated and powerful man. From considering Jesus as a blasphemous impostor he came to write of him as one 'who had no sin'
(2 Corinthians 5:21) — an astonishing confession from someone who had been such a violent persecutor of Jesus' followers.

We have similar statements from the writer of Hebrews. We
have already noticed his claim that Jesus was 'without sin'
(Hebrews 4:15). Later on, he adds that Jesus was 'holy, blame-
less, pure, set apart from sinners' (Hebrews 7:26) — words that
seem deliberately calculated to cover every possible angle of
approach — and that he 'offered himself unblemished to God'
(Hebrews 9:14). We need to bear in mind that in holding to
these beliefs those early followers of Jesus were risking their
own lives. Paul, for example, was flogged, tortured, imprisoned,

stoned, beaten up and, in his own words, 'exposed to death again and again' (2 Corinthians 11:23), yet he never flinched from his conviction that, far from being a blasphemous deceiver, Jesus had no sin of any kind. Paul was almost certainly executed by the Romans and countless others were killed for the same cause. Their deaths speak volumes. Do you hear what they are saying?

The inner circle

Of course, some would argue that these people never actually met Jesus; they were just attracted to an idea and ran with it. Then let us turn to *people who did know Jesus*, and knew him well. Early in his public ministry Jesus chose twelve disciples as his original followers. From these he picked three men — Peter, James and John — to be a kind of 'inner circle' and it is from them that we get the third tranche of evidence about the character of Jesus. These men were with him continually for about three years. They saw him in public and in private, in times of popularity and of opposition, when he was exhilarated and when he was exhausted. They had over a thousand days in which to watch, listen and assess. Their testimony is therefore vitally important; the argument about hearsay evidence will not wash here! Of this inner circle of three, two wrote New Testament books[1] in which they testified about Jesus' character. Peter said that Jesus was 'without blemish or defect' (1 Peter 1:19) adding that 'he committed no sin, and no deceit was found in his mouth' (1 Peter 2:22). That last phrase is particularly striking, because sins of speech are probably the most common. As one scholar put it, 'Most of man's sins are in his words.'[2] The Bible records Peter himself as being guilty of sins of speech such as bragging and lying and it may be that his own weakness in this area made the purity and integrity of Jesus' speech so impressive to him.

John's testimony is especially important because five times he describes himself as 'the disciple whom Jesus loved' (John 21:7). As Jesus loved all the disciples, this must refer to a particularly intimate relationship, one that gave him an unparalleled opportunity to assess his character. What is John's verdict on Jesus? He calls him 'righteous' (1 John 2:29) — the same word, meaning 'upright in God's sight', that was used by the Roman soldier — and says that 'in him is no sin' (1 John 3:5). The testimony of Jesus' closest friends is concise and convincing.

The one exception

The next area of evidence for the sinlessness of Jesus is even more remarkable: *he himself claimed it.* Has anybody in history ever seriously and sanely made such a claim for himself? The rule seems to be that the closer a person is to God, the more aware he becomes of his own sinfulness. This comes across very clearly in the Bible. Israel's King David was one of the greatest men in the Old Testament, yet confessed, 'I have sinned greatly' (2 Samuel 24:10). Isaiah was among the greatest of the prophets, yet admitted, 'I am a man of unclean lips' (Isaiah 6:5). Job was the most upright man of his day, yet cried out, 'I despise myself and repent in dust and ashes' (Job 42:6). The New Testament picture is the same, and John summed it all up by saying, 'If we claim to be without sin, we deceive ourselves and the truth is not in us' (1 John 1:8).

The same picture emerges from church history. One of the most influential figures since Bible times was Augustine, who died in A.D. 430, but in his famous book *The Confessions* he says, 'I will now call to mind my past foulness, and the carnal corruptions of my soul.' John Calvin has had a massive theological influence for over 400 years, yet a few days before his death he wrote, 'All I have done has been worth nothing ... I am a miserable creature ... my vices have always displeased.'[3] John Bunyan, who wrote the spiritual masterpiece *Pilgrim's Progress*, called his autobiography *Grace Abounding to the Chief of Sinners*. John Wesley's preaching on holiness changed the face of England, one historian ranking him 'the greatest force of the eighteenth century',[4] yet on his deathbed his own assessment was 'I the chief of sinners am.'[5] Wesley's contemporary George Whitefield has been called 'the greatest preacher that England has ever produced',[6] but saw himself as 'a guilty, weak and helpless worm'.[7] Jonathan Edwards was possibly the finest theologian and philosopher America has ever known, and was once described as 'one of the most holy, humble and heavenly minded men the world has seen since the apostolic age';[8] yet he once wrote, 'When I look into my heart, and take a view of my wickedness, it looks like an abyss infinitely deeper than hell.'[9] David Brainerd, the godly young missionary who died before he was thirty, and whose *Journal* has become a devotional classic, wrote of walking alone one night when 'I had opened to me such a view of my sin that I feared the ground would cleave asunder under my feet, and become my grave, and send my soul quick to hell before I could get home.'[10] No wonder someone has written that 'A consciousness of sin is one of the characteristics of the saints.'[11]

But when we come to Jesus the picture is totally different, because he showed no consciousness whatever of personal sin. In the first place, he said quite openly of his relationship with God, 'I always do what pleases him' (John 8:29). His words could hardly be more comprehensive: not 'sometimes' but 'always'. Do you know of anyone else who could seriously make that claim? Jesus confirmed his conviction a few hours before his death when he prayed, 'I have brought you glory on earth by completing the work you gave me to do' (John 17:4).

Secondly, Jesus indicated his innocence by separating himself from his hearers when speaking about sin. In giving an illustration about prayer he said, 'If you, then, though you are evil, know how to give good gifts to your children…' (Matthew 7:11). We would expect a preacher to identify himself with his hearers and say, 'if *we*, then, though *we* are evil…' — then why did Jesus speak of 'you' and not 'we'? There is only one explanation: he believed that whereas everyone else's life was tainted by sin, his was not. When he taught his disciples what we now call 'the Lord's Prayer' he introduced it by saying, 'This is how *you* should pray' (Matthew 6:9), not 'This is how *we* should pray'. Why? Because 'the Lord's Prayer' includes the petition, 'Forgive us our debts [our sins]' and Jesus never needed to use those words.

Thirdly, Jesus claimed complete mastery over temptation. Referring to the devil as 'the prince of this world' he added, 'He has no hold on me' (John 14:30). He was saying that there was nothing in his personality to which the devil could lay any claim or on which he could get any grip. Although the devil threw everything at him, he remained totally unscathed and unstained. He never blushed with shame, never had a guilty conscience, never regretted anything he did, never apologized.

Put all of that evidence together and you come up with this: if Jesus was not sinless, then he was the worst deceiver imaginable. As C. E. Jefferson puts it, 'The best reason we have for believing in the sinlessness of Jesus is the fact that he allowed his dearest friends to think that he was.'[12]

A word from heaven

But there is one even more convincing piece of evidence about the sinlessness of Jesus, and that is that *God stated it*. Two of the most significant events in the life of Jesus were his baptism and his transfiguration. Quite apart from their particular relevance, both occasions were marked by a phenomenon not repeated anywhere else in the gospel narrative: God spoke from heaven in a voice heard on earth. At his baptism, the words were directed to Jesus: 'You are my Son, whom I love; *with you I am well pleased*' (Luke 3:22). At his transfiguration (a remarkable event in which his whole appearance glowed with light) they were addressed to Peter, James and John, the 'inner circle': 'This is my Son, whom I love; *with him I am well pleased. Listen to him!*' (Matthew 17:5). Notice the words I have emphasized, because they are the exact opposite of God's assessment of the rest of humanity. We are told that after man's fall into sin 'God saw how corrupt the earth had become, for all the people on earth had corrupted their ways' (Genesis 6:12). Halfway through the Old Testament things were no better: 'Everyone has turned away, they have together become corrupt; there is no one who does good, not even one' (Psalm 53:3). A thousand years later, nothing had changed; God still declared, 'All have sinned and fall short of the glory of God' (Romans 3:23).

Yet on both these occasions God said of this thirty-year-old man, who had passed through all the traumas of growing up in a godless world surrounded by the pressure to conform to contemporary morality, something he never said of anyone else, that he was 'well pleased' with him. The words mean much more than pleasure at performance (such as parents might have when their child passes an examination). They imply that Jesus was everything that his heavenly Father wanted him to be, that he fulfilled to perfection God's plan for his life. Could anyone possibly have a greater endorsement than that?

The case against Jesus

What can be said against that avalanche of evidence? As far as I know, 2,000 years of analysis and investigation have produced only three charges to suggest that Jesus ever did anything wrong, and all three can be demolished without difficulty.

The first concerns Jesus driving people out of the temple at Jerusalem — and the allegation is that he sinned by losing his temper and allowing himself to get angry. There were two of these incidents, but they are so similar that one will serve to illustrate both.

'Jesus entered the temple area and drove out all who were buying and selling there. He overturned the tables of the money-changers and the benches of those selling doves. "It is written," he said to them, "'My house will be called a house of prayer,' but you are making it a 'den of robbers'"' (Matthew 21:12-13).

The temple at Jerusalem was the focal point of Jewish religious life, and people flocked to it from all over the world, particularly for special events. The Old Testament laid down very strict quality control on sacrifices to be offered at the temple, and this opened the door to all kinds of chicanery and corruption. A farmer might bring his best cow or sheep, only for one of the priests, acting as an inspector, to rule it unacceptable. The only place for the farmer to buy a suitable animal was from one of the merchants operating a concession (hand in glove with the priests of course) in one of the outer courts of the temple. Anxious to get to worship, the farmer would pay up, giving the merchant a nice profit and the priests their agreed percentage. Some of those selling doves were in on the same kind of deal at the lower end of the market (the law said that people could offer doves if they could not afford cattle). Many of the money-changers were also on to a good thing. Every Jew had to pay an annual temple tax, but it could only be paid in certain specified currencies. Needless to say, *bureaux de change* were right on the spot and would be delighted — for an extortionate commission — to oblige those who needed to get hold of some.

This was too much for Jesus. He overturned their tables and drove them out, reminding them that they had turned God's 'house of prayer' into a 'den or robbers'. Was Jesus angry? Yes, he was. Did he sin? No, he did not! As I was preparing to write this book, terrorists in Northern Ireland detonated a bomb that killed thirteen people on their way to an Armistice Day service in the town of Enniskillen. That made me angry! As I began this chapter, news came through of two sisters, one seventy-seven years of age and the other eighty-seven, who were attacked at their 'corner shop' home in the Midlands; one was smothered to death, the other strangled. That made me angry! As I write these words, I hear of an eighty-one-year old widow battered and then burned to death in her little terraced house in South Wales. That makes me angry! Surely any civilized human being should be angry when he hears of terrorism, violence, sadism, cruelty and other expressions of 'man's inhumanity to man'? As Dr Martyn Lloyd-Jones put it, 'The capacity for anger against that which is evil and wrong is something which is essentially right and good.'[13]

In fact, the Bible actually *commands* us to be angry! Writing to the church at Ephesus, Paul says, 'Be angry, and yet do not sin' (Ephesians 4:25, NASB)[14] and in that one sentence he shows us both the duty and danger of anger. We all know the second of these — someone has cleverly said that 'anger' is only one letter short of 'danger' — but most people have forgotten that there are times when anger is a duty. Righteous anger is a God-given capacity which we are meant to exercise in standing out against evil, and there is something radically deficient in a person who never has the courage to do so.

But the clearest reason for saying that anger is not necessarily wrong is that *God gets angry!* The Bible tells us of cities like Sodom and Gomorrah 'which the LORD overthrew in fierce anger' (Deuteronomy 29:23) and that God 'expresses his wrath every day' (Psalm 7:11). In the very nature of things, God's anger must be both holy and justifiable, and if God expresses anger at sin, Jesus can hardly be accused of sinning when he does the same thing!

The fruitless fig tree

The second charge is that Jesus lost his temper just because at a time when he was hungry he came across a fig tree with no fruit on it. This is Matthew's account of the incident: 'Early in the morning, as he was on his way back to the city, he was hungry. Seeing a fig tree by the road, he went up to it but found nothing on it except leaves. Then he said to it, "May you never bear fruit again!" Immediately the tree withered' (Matthew 21:18-19). On the surface, this might seem to have been a bad-tempered outburst — but was it?

That time of the year (around mid-April) was too early for full-grown figs, and Jesus would not expect to find any, but neither did he find any of the little green knobs (called *taqsh*) which appeared earlier and were also edible. This particular tree had 'nothing on it except leaves' — a sure sign that it was diseased in some way and would not bear any figs that year. Jesus then said, 'May you never bear fruit again!' There is no record of him ranting and raving, losing his temper, or attacking the tree in any way. He made one simple statement, and the tree withered away and died. What was wrong with that? Do we think that a person who uses a chain saw to cut down a tree or a spade to dig up a bush is doing something *evil*? And incidentally, do you know of anybody who can cause bushes to wither and die just by telling them to do so? If I thought the weeds in my garden would react like that, I would be glad to have a word with them! This incident certainly shows Jesus to be someone *special*; in no way does it show that he was sinful.

The whole point of the incident is its *meaning*. The Bible often uses the fig tree as a symbol of the people of Israel. God intended Israel to be spiritually fruitful, but by Jesus' time its religious system had become corrupt and had 'nothing on it except leaves'. It was full of outward rituals and ceremonies and lip-service, but barren when it came to godliness and true spirituality. In doing what he did to the fig tree, Jesus was forecasting the downfall of Israel and the coming of a time when 'the kingdom of God will be taken away from you and given to a people who will produce its fruit' (Matthew 21:43). This is exactly what happened in the passing away of the old order and the foundation of the Christian church.

Before leaving this incident, it is worth noting that this is the only time when Jesus did anything of this kind as an act of judgement, and that in mercy to man he chose to perform it on a lifeless object. His action was certainly miraculous, but by no stretch of the imagination could it be called malicious.

Goodness and God

The third charge concerns a discussion between Jesus and a rich young man. Mark records it like this: 'As Jesus started on his way, a man ran up to him and fell on his knees before him. "Good teacher," he asked, "what must I do to inherit eternal life?" "Why do you call me good?" Jesus answered. "No one is good — except God alone"' (Mark 10:17-18). The allegation here is that in saying 'No one is good — except God alone,' Jesus was admitting that he himself was *not* good, in other words that he too was a sinner. Again, the charge seems perfectly fair, but does it stand up to examination?

The first thing to be said is that if Jesus did admit that he was a sinner he contradicted every other statement he ever made about his own character. As we saw earlier, he repeatedly and unmistakably claimed to live a life that was utterly perfect, one which met all of God's requirements. A contradiction at this one point makes no sense at all.

The second thing to notice is that to treat the words of Jesus as an admission of his sinfulness is to isolate them from the whole context of the passage, because *it was not his character that was under discussion, but that of the other man.* Notice what happened. When the man addressed Jesus as 'Good teacher' he was using the word 'good' in a rather superficial way. He might even have been doing no more than complimenting Jesus on the quality of his teaching or his ability as a teacher. He was certainly not making any comment on Jesus' *character.* Jesus immediately took up his use of the word 'good' but deflected attention away from himself by pointing the man to God and to the commandments, which were a written reflection of God's character. Jesus pressed home his point by reminding him of the last six commandments (those concerning human relationships), to which he proudly replied, 'All these I have kept since I was a boy' (Mark 10:20). He obviously had a high opinion of his own character (he certainly thought *he* was good!) but a very superficial view of God's law. He had no idea that it went beyond outward actions and extended to thoughts, affections and desires. He had such a low view of God's law that he genuinely felt he was not guilty of breaking it.

Jesus then told him to sell all his possessions and give the proceeds to the poor and 'At this the man's face fell. He went away sad, because he had great wealth' (Mark 10:22). That one test showed his goodness to be superficial and selective. Even worse, he was in fact breaking the very first commandment: 'You shall have no other gods before me' (Exodus 20:3).

I have deliberately gone through the whole incident to emphasize one point: *it had nothing to do with the character of Jesus.* The young man never referred to it; nor did Jesus himself. The whole point of his opening remark was to show this earnest but mistaken young man that none of man's attempts at being 'good' could possibly measure up to God's requirements, nor could he ever get right with God by his own efforts.

When we examine it closely, the case against Jesus leaks like a sieve. Instead, all the evidence points to a man whose character is unique in human culture. He was not merely the finest; he was flawless. As Michael Green puts it, 'Every conceivable virtue known to man is there in him'[15] — and the more you read of his life the more you see that all of his qualities were held in perfect balance. Robert Clarke has rightly given this assessment of Jesus' character: 'There was meekness without weakness; tenderness without feebleness; firmness without coarseness; love without sentimentality; holiness without sanctimoniousness; lowliness without lowness; truth without error; enthusiasm without fanaticism; passion without prejudice; heavenly-mindedness without forgetfulness; carefreeness without carelessness; service without servility; self-exultation without egotism; judgement without harshness; seriousness without sombreness; mercy without softness.'[16]

Faced with some of his religious critics one day, Jesus asked, 'Can any of you prove me guilty of sin?' (John 8:46). That question was not answered at the time. It has never been answered since.

6.

The man who died twice

When the Irish writer George Bernard Shaw completed a statistical study on the subject of death he came to only one firm conclusion: 'one out of one dies'. That is why biographers seldom spend much time on the death of their subjects. There may be considerable mileage in how a person died (volumes have been written on the assassination of United States President John F. Kennedy in 1963) or there may be glowing tributes to a brave fight against pain, or interesting details of the subject's final hours, but death itself is never an issue because it is inevitable. In the Bible's words, 'Man is destined to die' (Hebrews 9:27); death is usually no more than the obvious end of the biographer's story.

The main thing

Yet even this rule is broken when we come to Jesus of Nazareth, because about one third of the 'Gospels' (the first four books of the New Testament, and the closest we get to a biography of Jesus) is devoted to the events surrounding his death. The apostle Paul, who wrote most of the rest of the New Testament, summed up his ministry with the words, 'We preach Christ crucified' (1 Corinthians 1:23), and reminded friends, 'I resolved to know nothing while I was with you except Jesus Christ and him crucified' (1 Corinthians 2:2). To others he wrote, 'May I never boast except in the cross of our Lord Jesus Christ' (Galatians 6:14). It is no exaggeration to say with Dr Leon Morris that 'The cross dominates the New Testament.'[1] This is remarkable when we remember that the cross was grossly offensive to the three major cultures of that time. To the Romans, it was so despicable that the republican orator and statesman Cicero wrote, 'Even the mere word "cross" must remain far not only from the lips of the citizens of Rome, but also from their thoughts, their eyes, their ears.'[2] To the Jews, crucifixion was in the same category as hanging, and the Old Testament went so far as to say that 'Anyone who is hung on a tree is under God's curse' (Deuteronomy 21:23). To the Greeks, the subject made no sense at all, so that when Paul insisted that the death of Jesus was important, they wrote the whole idea off as 'absurd and utterly unphilosophical nonsense' (1 Corinthians 1:23, Amplified Bible).

Yet Jesus constantly emphasized the centrality of his crucifixion. Time and time again he warned his disciples what would happen to him, and eventually became quite specific: '"We are going up to Jerusalem," he said, "and the Son of Man will be betrayed to the chief priests and teachers of the law. They will condemn him to death and will hand him over to the Gentiles, who will mock him and spit on him, flog him and kill him"' (Mark 10:33-34). But he went further; he spoke of his death as being the climax of his life rather than merely its conclusion. When he was catapulted into the limelight at the beginning of his public ministry he said, 'My time has not yet come' (John 2:4). On separate occasions two years later life-threatening situations came to nothing 'because his time had not yet come' (John 7:30; 8:20). But a few days before his death his language suddenly changed. When Greek visitors to Jerusalem asked to see him, Jesus said, 'The hour has come for the Son of Man to be glorified', adding later, 'Now my heart is troubled, and what shall I say? "Father, save me from this hour"? No, it was for this *very reason I came to this hour'* (John 12:23,27). Then on the night of his arrest he prayed, 'Father, *the time has come'* (John 17:1). All the past was prologue. Within a few hours he would be killed, but his death would not conclude his purpose for coming into the world; it would crown it. In John Stott's phrase, 'The hour for which he had come into the world was the hour in which he left it.'[3]

It is fascinating to discover what some people rate as life's crowning achievement. Some years ago Associated Press ran the story of an eighty-eight-year-old British peer who had devoted his life to trying to breed the perfect spotted mouse! While I was once in Greece the local press announced the death of a well-known bishop of the Greek Orthodox Church, and praised him to the skies for his greatest achievement: he had the bones of St Andrew moved from Italy to Greece! Others are noted for more significant achievements than mating rodents or moving remains — military conquests, scientific discoveries, the exploration of earth or space, social reform, political leadership and the like — but according to the Bible the most significant thing Jesus did was to die! Two thousand years later the universally recognized symbol of the movement he began is not a reminder of his unique conception, his sinless character, his matchless teaching or his remarkable miracles, but a cross — the cruellest instrument of execution known to the ancient world.

Cause of death

Nobody can argue with the statement that death is universal and inevitable, and we are powerless to prevent it. As the seventeenth-century preacher Thomas Brooks wrote to a friend, 'As many pores as there are in the body, so many windows there are for death to enter at.'[4] The best that the greatest of medical marvels can do is to postpone the inevitable. Nobody has to

ask the question, 'Is there death after life?' — but everybody
ought to ask another question: *'Why?'* Why is it that every human
being, of whatever race, colour or creed, has to face what J. I.
Packer calls this 'malevolent monstrosity'?[5] Put another way,
what *causes* death? It is not enough to talk about the heart
stopping, the lungs collapsing, or the brain ceasing to function;
those are legitimate medical concepts, but they get us no nearer
to a satisfying answer to the question. If we go a step further we
could say that there are just four ways of dying: execution (law-
ful or unlawful), suicide, accidental death, and what we call
'natural causes'. But does that help us? I worked for several
years in the Registrar-General's Office on the Channel Island of
Guernsey, where one of my jobs was to write out copies of
death certificates. Although I wrote hundreds of them in my
time there I can still remember the chilling emotion I often felt
when filling in the column headed 'Cause of Death'. Sometimes the words were frighteningly long, such as 'arterioscler-
otic degeneration of the myocardium'; at other times they were
bleakly brief: 'cancer'. Yet I hardly ever completed that particular column without reflecting that a human life, with all its powers
and potential, had suddenly been brought to an end. But even
when we have waded through an encyclopaedia of diseases
we have only discovered *how* people die. We have still not
answered the deeper question, 'Why?' To do so, we must turn
to the Bible.

Back to the beginning

The first mention of death comes very early in the Bible's history of mankind, *but not at the very beginning.* Man was originally created 'in the image of God' (Genesis 1:27). He was morally
and spiritually perfect, stamped with God's holy character, and
lived in a state of moral and spiritual perfection in a perfect

world and in total harmony with his Creator. But God made it clear to him that this state of affairs was conditional. Man, and the equally perfect wife God had provided for him, had been placed in a beautiful and bountiful environment containing everything necessary for their enrichment and enjoyment, but it was all subject to one condition: *their total and unqualified obedience.* (Technically, this arrangement is known as 'the covenant of works'.) The Bible records man's privilege and God's proviso like this: 'And the LORD God commanded the man, "You are free to eat from any tree in the garden; but you must not eat from the tree of the knowledge of good and evil, for when you eat of it you will surely *die*"' (Genesis 2:16-17). It was the first time man had ever heard the word.

Whatever this 'tree of the knowledge of good and evil' was, man was given a straightforward test of his willingness to do what God said *simply because God said it.* It was a clear-cut issue of God's right to command and man's duty to obey — and man failed the test. Tempted by the devil to question God's command, the woman could not resist the attraction of what God had forbidden: 'The woman saw that the fruit of the tree was good for food and pleasing to the eye, and also desirable for gaining wisdom...' (Genesis 3:6). The picture is brilliantly clear. The fruit of the tree appealed first to her physical appetite (it was 'good for food'), then to her aesthetic taste (it was 'pleasing to the eye'), then to her intellectual ambition (it was 'desirable for gaining wisdom') and the longer she thought about it the more her resistance crumbled; as someone has said, she 'followed her impressions against her instructions'[6] and in next to no time the damage was done: 'She took some and ate it. She also gave some to her husband, who was with her, and he ate it' (Genesis 3:6).

God had warned Adam and Eve that disobedience would immediately lead to death, and it did, even though they went on living for many years. This apparent contradiction is unravelled by the fact that *the basic meaning of 'death' is not termination but separation*. The Bible speaks not only of physical death (the separation of the soul from the body) but also of spiritual death (the separation of the soul from God). When we grasp this, we are in a position to understand what happened to Adam and Eve. The moment they sinned, they died spiritually; their relationship with God was shattered. Instead of welcoming the sound of his voice and the assurance of his presence, 'they hid from the LORD God among the trees of the garden' (Genesis 3:8), guilty, ashamed and afraid. But that was not all: from the moment of that first sin they became subject to disease, decay and deterioration, leading inevitably to physical death.

The lethal law

Far from being nothing more than ancient history, the fatal outcome of Adam's disobedience is right up to date, because his corrupt nature was passed on not only to his children, who were born 'in his own likeness, in his own image' (Genesis 5:3), but through them to every subsequent generation. Put very simply, Adam *became* a sinner; you and I were *born* that way. The depravity and corruption of sin were built into our natures just as surely as genes and chromosomes were built into our genetic make-up. King David of Israel, one of the greatest men in the Old Testament, got it absolutely right when he said, 'Surely I was sinful at birth, sinful from the time my mother conceived me' (Psalm 51:5). This built-in bias is sometimes called 'original sin', and it is this which leads to all the acts of sin which pollute and ruin our lives and to the inevitable penalty they incur.

To make matters worse, we share Adam's *guilt* as well as his corruption and pollution, because Adam was mankind's representative. Paul emphasizes this terrible truth by saying, 'Sin entered the world through one man, and death through sin, and in this way death came to all men, because all sinned' (Romans 5:12). Moments later he adds that 'many died by the trespass of the one man' (Romans 5:15), that 'judgement followed one sin and brought condemnation' (Romans 5:16) and that 'the result of one trespass was condemnation for all men' (Romans 5:18). By his sin, Adam ruined all those he represented, and the evidence of man's inherent spiritual death is his inevitable physical death.

This link between sin and death pervades the whole Bible: 'The soul who sins is the one who will die' (Ezekiel 18:20). 'He who pursues evil goes to his death' (Proverbs 11:19). 'The wages of sin is death' (Romans 6:23). 'Sin, when it is full-grown, gives birth to death' (James 1:15). The link between the two is so fixed and fundamental that the Bible calls it 'the law of sin and death' (Romans 8:2). This law is part of the moral fabric of the universe, as fixed and fundamental as the law of gravity. Death is God's righteous and inescapable punishment of human sin. Before man sinned, death was impossible; since he sinned, it is inevitable, and not one single sin — of word, thought or deed — can ever avoid it.

As if that were not serious enough, the Bible adds one final clause to the lethal law of sin and death; it says a person remaining separated from God until the end of life will be 'punished with everlasting destruction and shut out from the presence of the Lord and from the majesty of his power' (2 Thessalonians 1:9). The Bible's most common word for this is 'hell', the ultimate penalty for sin.

Having established that death is the inevitable outworking of a law of cause and effect, the death of Jesus presents us with a problem to which there appears to be no answer. As Jesus had no sin of any kind, and as it is sin that causes death, *why did he die?* The Bible has a clear and consistent answer to that question.

The voluntary victim

It is obvious that Jesus *ought* not to have died (or at least ought not to have been executed) because he was clearly innocent of all the false charges brought against him. We have also seen that in a deeper sense he had no *need* to die, because he was innocent of any sin of any kind. Yet he was mocked, flogged, stripped, tortured and eventually nailed to a wooden cross and left to hang there until he was dead. *Why?*

An important part of the Bible's answer to that question is that *he died of his own volition*. This makes the death of Jesus the only voluntary death in human history. But what about those who lose their lives trying to rescue others, or soldiers killed in acts of bravery against overwhelming odds, or people who commit suicide? The answer is that none of these *chooses* to die. In the first two cases (and all others like them) the most they do is to put their lives at risk, while suicides merely choose the day, the time, the place and the method of their death. Yet sooner or later they are all 'destined to die' (Hebrews 9:27). As someone has put it, 'All the world is a hospital, and every person in it a terminal patient.' Yet the New Testament makes it clear that Jesus *volunteered* to die, and we can pick up vital indications of this at various stages of his life.

There was at least a hint of it at his transfiguration: 'Two men, Moses and Elijah, appeared in glorious splendour, talking with Jesus. They spoke about his departure, which he was about to bring to fulfilment at Jerusalem' (Luke 9:31). His 'departure' (the original Greek word is *exodus*) obviously means his death, but it seems strange to speak of this as something 'he was about to bring to fulfilment'. Death was not going to *happen* to him; instead, he was going to bring it about. What is more, he would not throw his life away by committing suicide; instead, he would deliberately die in order to accomplish something. Later, in speaking of his purpose in coming into the world, he said, 'I am the good shepherd. The good shepherd lays down his life for the sheep' (John 10:11). The picture is not that of a shepherd who takes one risk too many in protecting his flock, because Jesus went on to say, 'No one takes [my life] from me, but I lay it down of my own accord' (John 10:18). His meaning could not have been clearer. He would not merely risk his life, but deliberately give it up.

Later still, warning his disciples about the danger of selfish ambition, Jesus said that 'even the Son of Man did not come to be served, but to serve, and to give his life as a ransom for many' (Mark 10:45). We will look at the word 'ransom' later, but notice that Jesus spoke of *giving* his life — a deliberate act of laying it down and giving it up.

When he was eventually arrested, one of his followers attacked the high priest's servant with a sword and sliced off one of his ears. Telling him to put his sword away, Jesus asked, 'Do you think I cannot call on my Father, and he will at once put at my disposal more than twelve legions of angels?' (Matthew 26:53). A Roman legion consisted of about 6,000 men, and an Old Testament incident records one angel annihilating 185,000 soldiers in a single night; twelve legions of them could easily have wiped out over thirteen million people — more than the entire population of the world at that time. But it is not a matter of mathematics: the real point is that Jesus could have escaped at any time he wished, *and he chose not to*.

Other powerful evidence comes at the very moment Jesus died: 'And when Jesus had cried out again in a loud voice, *he gave up his spirit*' (Matthew 27:50). Whatever we may think about medical definitions of the exact moment of death, it would be precisely accurate to say that death comes when the spirit leaves the body. This fits in perfectly with what we observe. As J. I. Packer remarks, 'It is sometimes said that the dead look peaceful, but this is hardly correct. What is true is that the dead look *vacant.'*[7] Sometimes the spirit leaves peacefully, while the person concerned is asleep. Sometimes it is violently removed. Sometimes there is an agonizing battle as the sufferer struggles to hold on to life. Take the case of Joseph Stalin, the Russian dictator who died in 1953. Here is part of a moving description of his last moments given by his daughter, Svetlana Alliluyeva: 'The death agony was horrible. He literally choked to death. At what seemed like the very last moment he suddenly opened his eyes and cast a glance over everyone in the room. It was a terrible glance, insane, or perhaps angry, and full of fear of death and the unfamiliar faces of the doctors bent over him. The glance swept over everyone in a second. Then something incomprehensible and awesome happened, that to this day I can't forget and don't understand. He suddenly lifted his left hand as though bringing down a curse on us all. The gesture was incomprehensible and full of menace, and no one could say to whom or what it might be directed. The next moment, after a final effort, *the spirit wrenched itself free of the flesh.'*[8]

The death of Jesus was very different. There was no wrenching of the spirit from the flesh; instead, Jesus '*gave up* his spirit'. The literal meaning is that he 'sent it away', like a master dismissing a servant. But the Bible specifically states that 'No man has power to retain the spirit, or authority over the day of death' (Ecclesiastes 8:8, Revised Standard Version, see NIV footnote). If a man could prevent the spirit leaving the body, he could make himself immortal; if he could dismiss his spirit by an act of the will, suicide would be simple and serene. Yet once again Jesus is the exception to the rule. He deliberately, clearly and intelligently dismissed his spirit. He was not drugged (he refused the crude anaesthetic offered to him), and he still had the strength to 'cry out again in a loud voice'. Simply put, he had complete authority over the moment of his death. He died not only by crucifixion, but by choice. In Augustine's words, 'He gave up his life *because* he willed it, *when* he willed it, and *as* he willed it.'[9]

The man for others

Having established that Jesus volunteered to die, we still face the major problem of *how* he could have died if death results from sin and he never sinned. That leads us to another layer of truth from the Bible, which is that when Jesus died he did so *on behalf of others and in their place*. However staggering that may seem, the Bible's evidence about this is clear and consistent. Some of the next quotations will include other important truths that we will examine later in this chapter, but for the moment I will emphasize in italics the one point that in his death Jesus acted as a substitute, taking the place of sinners.

At a last meal with his followers, he told them that the cup of wine was a symbol of his own blood, 'which is poured out *for many* for the forgiveness of sins' (Matthew 26:28), a clear indication that he was speaking of himself as a substitute, taking the place of other people. The same truth was one of Paul's main themes: 'Christ died for the ungodly' (Romans 5:6); 'While we were still sinners, Christ died *for us*' (Romans 5:8); 'God made him who had no sin to be sin *for us*' (2 Corinthians 5:21); 'He died *for us*' (1 Thessalonians 5:10). The apostle Peter was just as insistent: 'Christ suffered *for you*' (1 Peter 2:21); 'He himself bore *our* sins in his body on the tree' (1 Peter 2:24); 'For Christ died for sins once for all, *the righteous for the unrighteous*, to bring you to God' (1 Peter 3:18). The apostle John agreed: 'Jesus Christ laid down his life *for us*' (1 John 3:16); 'God ... sent his Son as an atoning sacrifice *for our sins*' (1 John 4:10). Robert Clarke is right when he says that 'In the New Testament the truth of substitution stands out so clearly it cannot be got rid of without getting rid of the book itself.'[10]

The Old and the New

But it is not only the New Testament that says that Jesus died in the place of others. One of the most important chapters in the Old Testament is Isaiah 53, which speaks of a suffering servant who would bear the sins of others and die in their place. During that final meal with his disciples, Jesus quoted from Isaiah 53 and added, 'Yes, what is written about me is reaching its fulfilment' (Luke 22:37). New Testament writers agreed, and had no doubt that Jesus was the 'servant' foretold by Isaiah. When Jesus healed the sick, Matthew commented, 'This was to fulfil what was spoken through the prophet Isaiah: "He took up our infirmities and carried our diseases"' (Matthew 8:17). When people refused to believe in Jesus in spite of the miracles he was performing, John wrote, 'This was to fulfil the word of Isaiah the prophet: "Lord, who has believed our message and to whom has the arm of the Lord been revealed?"' (John 12:38).

At other times, they obviously wrote about Jesus with the same Old Testament prophecy in mind. This passage written by Peter has no fewer than six phrases lifted from Isaiah 53: '"He committed no sin, and no deceit was found in his mouth." When they hurled their insults at him, *he did not retaliate*; when he suffered, *he made no threats*. Instead, he entrusted himself to him who judges justly. *He himself bore our sins* in his body on the tree, so that we might die to sins and live for righteousness; *by his wounds you have been healed. For you were like sheep going astray*, but now you have returned to the Shepherd and Overseer of your souls' (1 Peter 2:22-25).

Then there was an occasion when Philip the evangelist came across a high-ranking government official from Ethiopia who was reading Isaiah 53, but without a clue as to what it meant. When he asked of whom the prophet was speaking, 'Philip began with that very passage of Scripture and told him the good news about Jesus' (Acts 8:35).

Yet this is still not the whole picture. Here is another passage from Isaiah 53 that clearly matches the New Testament's insistence that Jesus died as a substitute for sinners:

'But he was pierced for our transgressions,
    he was crushed for our iniquities;
the punishment that brought us peace was upon him,
    and by his wounds we are healed.
We all, like sheep, have gone astray,
    each of us has turned to his own way;
and the LORD has laid on him
    the iniquity of us all'

(Isaiah 53:5-6).

Of the seventeen sentences in Isaiah 53, no fewer than sixteen are applied to Jesus in the New Testament, some of them several times, and the remaining one (which speaks of the suffering servant's unattractive personal appearance) would certainly have been true of Jesus when the Roman soldiers had finished with him. The whole passage has the unmistakable ring of truth — the truth that Jesus, the Messiah, offered up his life as a substitutionary sacrifice for the sins of others. The nineteenth-century Bible commentator Albert Barnes put it like this: 'It would be impossible to state in more explicit language the truth that [Jesus] died as a sacrifice for the sins of men; that he suffered to make proper expiation for the guilty. No confession of faith on earth, no creed, no symbol, no standard of doctrine, contains more explicit statements on the subject.'[11]

The other 'Why?'

So far we have seen that death is the result of sin, but that Jesus, who had no sin, died in the place of others, as their substitute. We can now begin to answer some very big questions, but before we do so, let me tackle one issue that needs to be handled at this point. Many people accept that in some way Jesus died *on behalf* of others, without accepting that he died *in their place*. If asked why Jesus died, these people say that he died as an example. Is that true? And is it the whole truth? The Bible certainly gives a clear answer to the first question: 'Christ suffered for you, leaving you an example, that you should follow in his steps' (1 Peter 2:21). This phrase is part of a section from which I quoted a few paragraphs ago, and it is important to understand its context. The early Christians were suffering a great deal of persecution, especially at the hands of the pagan Emperor Nero and others. Jesus had predicted this: 'If they persecuted me, they will persecute you also... They will treat you this way because of my name' (John 15:20-21). Now that his words were coming true, what should his followers do? How should they react to oppression, injustice, violence? Peter points them straight to Jesus himself — and the inference is obvious. If they would follow his example, they must not attack their attackers, nor meet violence with violence or injustice with injustice. Instead, they must faithfully commit their cause to God, just as Jesus 'entrusted himself to him who judges justly' (1 Peter 2:23).

So it is certainly true to say that in his suffering and death Jesus was a marvellous example of meekness, forbearance, forgiveness and faith — and equally true to say that his example remains an uncomfortable challenge in a world where men's normal reaction is not submission but assertion, not just to 'get mad' but to 'get even'. But this is far from the main thing we see in the death of Jesus; in fact, there is virtually no other place in the New Testament where his suffering and death are said to be an example. This is not surprising, because it would be impossible to explain most of the Gospel narrative in those terms. For instance, Jesus spoke of his death as being 'for the forgiveness of sins' (Matthew 26:28), but how could an example achieve that? As John Stott says, 'A pattern cannot secure our pardon... An example can stir our imagination, kindle our idealism and strengthen our resolve, but it cannot cleanse the defilement of our past sins, bring peace to our troubled conscience or fetch us home to God.'[12] The death of Jesus *was* an example, but it was much more than that.

The big words

It is becoming more and more obvious as we go along that the death of Jesus had a specific purpose. It demands an explanation beyond that which accounts for the death of any other human being. What was that purpose? We brushed against it a few pages ago in Peter's statement that 'Christ died for sins once for all, the righteous for the unrighteous, *to bring you to God*' (1 Peter 3:18). I cannot think of a single phrase anywhere in the New Testament that puts it more precisely than that. To explain how this was accomplished we must tackle several major technical words. It would be much easier to ignore them, but if we are really serious in our search for the real Jesus we must try to get a grasp of what they mean.

Satisfying God

The first of our 'big words' is '*propitiation*'. It occurs three times in older English versions of the Bible, but as it is hardly an everyday word, the translators of the New International Version (which I am using almost exclusively in this book) have tried to clarify its meaning by using a different phrase. Here are the three references: 'God presented [Jesus] as a *sacrifice of atonement*, through faith in his blood' (Romans 3:25); '[Jesus] is *the atoning sacrifice* for our sins…' (1 John 2:2); 'This is love: not that we loved God, but that he loved us and sent his Son as *an atoning sacrifice* for our sins' (1 John 4:10). These phrases help, but they still fall short of the full meaning. 'Propitiation' means appeasing an offended person by meeting his demands for the removal of an offence, and as a result enabling the offender to win back his favour. This gives us our first insight into what Jesus accomplished by his death. To think of God only in terms of kindness, love and mercy gives an unbalanced picture, because the Bible also speaks of his 'fierce anger' (Deuteronomy 29:23) and says that 'God … expresses his wrath every day' (Psalm 7:11). Elsewhere, it tells us why God is angry: 'The wrath of God is being revealed from heaven against all the godlessness and wickedness of men who suppress the truth by their wickedness…' (Romans 1:18); 'God's wrath comes on those who are disobedient' (Ephesians 5:6). Many people today have a sentimental view of God, but a careful scholar like A. W. Pink says that in the Bible 'There are more references to the anger, fury and wrath of God than there are to his love and tenderness.'[13]

Yet God's anger is never bad-tempered, misplaced, 'over the top', malicious or vindictive — as ours often is. Instead, it is perfectly righteous, his proper, personal and holy reaction against sin. It is also perfectly fair — the outworking of man's sinful choice. As Jesus put it, 'Light has come into the world, but men loved darkness instead of light because their deeds were evil' (John 3:19). If men prefer sin to holiness and God's absence to his presence, they can hardly complain at the outcome. In J. I. Packer's words, 'The essence of God's action in wrath is to *give men what they choose*, in all its implications: nothing more, and equally nothing less.'[14] Those implications are horrifying. There can be nothing worse in this life than being exposed to God's anger (as every sinner is) and to be 'storing up wrath against yourself for the day of God's wrath, when his righteous judgement will be revealed' (Romans 2:5).

It is exactly here that the death of Jesus meets sinners at their point of need. In becoming an atoning sacrifice (a 'propitiation') in the place of others, Jesus took upon himself the consequences of God's anger against their sin, and in so doing turned it away from them and made it possible for God to act favourably towards them.

Purchased at a price

The fact that Jesus appeased God's anger at the cost of his own life leads us directly to the next two technical words — *ransom* and *redemption*.

At the beginning of this chapter we saw that sin separates man from God, but that is not the whole picture. The Bible also teaches that the sinner is not just a castaway but a captive. In the Old Testament we read that 'The evil deeds of a wicked man ensnare him' (Proverbs 5:22). Jesus underlines this: 'I tell you the truth, everyone who sins is a slave to sin' (John 8:34). Paul speaks about people being 'slaves to sin' (Romans 6:16) and recalls a time when he had been 'a prisoner of the law of sin at work within my members' (Romans 7:23). Later, he goes even further and makes it clear that sinners are not merely in bondage to some vague principle but to the devil himself: they are in 'the trap of the devil, who has taken them captive' (2 Timothy 2:26). Far from having unlimited free will, with absolute liberty to choose between good and evil, man is a moral and spiritual prisoner. Not that that gives sinners an excuse for sinning because, as John Calvin says, 'They do nothing by constraint, but are inclined with their whole heart to that to which Satan drives them. The result is that their captivity is voluntary.'[15]

It is only when we appreciate the sinner's terrible position —
gladly submitting to slavery that is wrecking his life and leading
him to hell — that we can appreciate the words 'ransom' and
'redemption' when applied to the death of Jesus. A ransom is
the price paid for the release of a prisoner, while redemption is
setting a prisoner free by the payment of a ransom — and these
are exactly the meanings these words have in the Bible. When
Jesus said that he had come 'to give his life as a ransom for
many' (Mark 10:45) he meant that he would give his own sinless
life as the ransom price to divine justice in order to secure the
release of others; he would accept the penalty for their sin so
that they could be free from it. Other New Testament writers
underline this. Paul speaks of 'the redemption that came by
Christ Jesus' (Romans 3:24) and says that 'God sent his Son,
born of a woman, born under law, to redeem those under law'
(Galatians 4:4-5). Elsewhere he emphasizes the stupendous *cost*
involved in bringing about the prisoners' release, reminding his
friend Titus that Jesus 'gave himself for us to redeem us from
all wickedness' (Titus 2:14). Peter makes the same point: 'For
you know that it was not with perishable things such as silver or
gold that you were redeemed from the empty way of life handed
down to you from your forefathers, but with the precious blood
of Christ, a lamb without blemish or defect' (1 Peter 1:18-19).
To the Jews, the lamb was a symbol of patience, meekness and
gentleness, and all of these qualities applied to Jesus as he was
led to his execution, but Peter had much more than this in mind.
At the annual Passover feast, a lamb was killed and eaten to
commemorate the way in which God had delivered Israel from
over 400 years of captivity and slavery in Egypt. This would
have come across vividly to Peter's Jewish readers. The morally spotless Jesus shed his own blood to release others from
the captivity of sin. This is what John the Baptist meant when
he introduced Jesus as 'the Lamb of God, who takes away the

sin of the world!' (John 1:29) and what Paul had in mind when he said, 'Christ, our Passover lamb, has been sacrificed' (1 Corinthians 5:7).

But redemption through the death of Jesus brings about yet another benefit. Paul says that 'In [Jesus Christ] we have redemption through his blood, *the forgiveness of sins*' (Ephesians 1:7). Man as a sinner is guilty and in debt. Forgiveness by God releases him from both his guilt and his indebtedness, cutting him loose from its burden and setting him free to lead a new life. There is an illustration of this in John Bunyan's spiritual classic *Pilgrim's Progress*. This is how the narrator describes the turning point in the pilgrim's journey: 'He ran thus till he came to a place somewhat ascending; and upon that place stood a cross, and a little below, in the bottom, a sepulchre. So I saw in my dream that, just as Christian came up with the cross, his burden fell from off his back, and began to tumble, till it came to the mouth of the sepulchre, where it fell in, and I saw it no more.'[16]

Relationship restored

Our fourth word is *reconciliation*, which hardly needs to be explained but does need to be illustrated. As we saw earlier, man originally lived in perfect harmony with God, but as soon as he sinned that relationship was shattered. Not only did man show himself to be a rebel against God's holy will, and in that sense become God's enemy; he also offended and angered God, who in turn became his enemy. Ever since, a barrier made up of what we might call two 'thicknesses' — man's sinful rebellion and God's righteous anger — has separated God and man. Man is wrongly the enemy of God and God is rightly the enemy of man. Both of these truths are clearly stated in Scripture. In the first place we are told that 'The sinful mind is hostile to God' (Romans 8:7) and that 'Anyone who chooses to be a friend of the world becomes an enemy of God' (James 4:4). Left to himself, man remains a determined rebel; he hates God and everything he stands for. Even when God sent his Son to rescue helpless sinners they openly rejected him, so that Jesus could say, 'Light has come into the world, but men loved darkness instead of light because their deeds were evil' (John 3:19).

Yet the main emphasis in Scripture is on the fact that God has become man's enemy. We get an illustration of this soon after man sinned: 'The LORD God banished him from the Garden of Eden to work the ground from which he had been taken. After he drove the man out, he placed on the east side of the Garden of Eden cherubim and a flaming sword flashing back and forth to guard the way to the tree of life' (Genesis 3:23-24). Man was not only excluded from the garden, but the way back to it was barred. This shows us something of the awesome holiness of God, which banishes all unholiness from his presence. The Bible then goes on to give numerous instances of God expressing his enmity against man in his sin and rebellion, and on many other occasions it is stated as a general principle. We are told that God 'expresses his wrath every day' (Psalm 7:11) and that he 'takes vengeance on his foes and maintains his wrath against his enemies' (Nahum 1:2). Paul warns us, 'The wrath of God is being revealed from heaven against all the godlessness and wickedness of men' (Romans 1:18). God has continued to show his anger against sin in many ways in the course of human history. As Geoffrey Wilson says, 'God is no idle spectator of world events; he is dynamically active in human affairs. The commission of sin is punctuated by divine judgement.'[17] Anyone who cannot see that God has intervened in history to show his anger at man's sin should look again.

God also expresses his righteous anger at an individual and personal level, not least in man's conscience, which reminds

him of God's unchangeable standards and of man's wrong-
doing and guilt. What a mess man has got himself into! By his
own deliberate rebellion and self-centredness he has turned his
Creator into his enemy and placed himself under God's holy
anger, 'the reaction of the divine righteousness when it comes
into collision with sin'.[18]

Now comes the good news! In the death of Jesus, the innocent party (God) has done something stupendous to enable
the guilty party (man) to return in peace. Paul says that 'God
was reconciling the world to himself in Christ' (2 Corinthians
5:19). He tells another group of fellow-Christians, 'Once you
were alienated from God and were enemies in your minds because of your evil behaviour. But now he has reconciled you by
Christ's physical body through death to present you holy in his
sight, without blemish and free from accusation' (Colossians
1:21-22). There are two things to notice here. The first is that
God has taken the initiative. Man has neither the power nor the
inclination to do anything about the problem. In spite of all the
horrific effects of the enmity between him and God, he prefers
to keep things that way. He wants to run away from God, to
keep him at a distance. The second is that God has brought
about reconciliation by dealing with the root cause of the problem — man's sin. In the death of his Son, God punished human
sin and satisfied his own righteous judgement, Jesus taking upon
himself the sin, guilt and condemnation of those on whose behalf he died. In this way God removed the barrier which separated him from man, so that Paul can say, 'When we were God's
enemies, we were reconciled to him through the death of his
Son' (Romans 5:10).

It is against this background that the Bible issues this amazing invitation to guilty and rebellious sinners: 'Be reconciled to
God' (2 Corinthians 5:20). Here is an invitation to take advantage of God's astonishing love and to return to a living, joyful
relationship with him. The only thing more amazing than that
invitation is that most sinners refuse to accept it.

Right with God

The last of our 'big words' is *justification*, one of the greatest in the Bible. The simplest way to get at its meaning is to realize that it comes from the law courts. It is a word which pronounces a verdict, the declaration of a judge that the person standing before him is 'not liable to any penalty, but is entitled to all the privileges due to those who have kept the law'.[19] In other words, it is the exact opposite of condemnation, which declares a man to be guilty and sentences him to the penalty the law prescribes.

When we apply all this to man's position before God, it is not difficult to see that we are faced with a massive dilemma. How can a *righteous* God possibly declare guilty sinners to be 'not guilty' and to be acceptable in his sight, without bending the rules and compromising his own righteousness? Put the other way around, how can God punish sin (as he must) and yet declare the sinner free from guilt and its consequences? Only God could provide an answer to such questions, and the Bible says that he has done so in the life and death of his Son, Jesus Christ. There has been no bending of the rules. God is still inflexibly holy and just and utterly opposed to sin. He remains 'too pure to look on evil' and 'cannot tolerate wrong' (Habakkuk 1:13). Yet in the life and death of Jesus he has provided a way in which he can justify sinners.

God's law makes a double demand on men: as God's crea-tures, they must obey it in every part; as sinners, they must pay its penalty in full. Men have done neither — *but Jesus did both!* In his perfect life Jesus met all the righteous demands of God's holy law; he was able to say, 'The world must learn that I love the Father and that I do exactly what my Father has commanded me' (John 14:31). In his death, he paid in full the penalty God's law demands: 'Christ died for sins once for all, the righteous for the unrighteous' (1 Peter 3:18). Both in his life and in his death Jesus was acting on behalf of others and in their place. He lived the life they did not live and died the death they should have died. It is only when we grasp this that we can begin to understand the Bible's statements about justification — about sinners being right with God.

Here are just five of them. Firstly, nobody can get right with God by his or her own moral or spiritual efforts at keeping God's law: 'We ... know that a man is not justified by observing the law' (Galatians 2:16). Secondly, God has provided a way by which a person can be justified: 'But God demonstrates his own love for us in this: While we were still sinners, Christ died for us ... we have now been justified by his blood' (Romans 5:8-9). Thirdly, justification meets the demands of God's justice: 'God presented [Jesus] as a sacrifice of atonement, through faith in his blood. He did this ... to demonstrate his justice at the present time, so as to be just and the one who justifies those who have faith in Jesus' (Romans 3:25-26). Fourthly, God's gift of justification must be received by faith: 'For we maintain that a man is justified by faith apart from observing the law' (Romans 3:28). Fifthly, justification frees the sinner from sin's death penalty and brings him into a new, living relationship with God: 'Therefore, since we have been justified through faith, we have peace with God through our Lord Jesus Christ' (Romans 5:1).

What amazing truth this is! Justification is more than being forgiven; it is being brought into favour with God, as if we had met all the demands of his holy law. Dr Leon Morris has put it like this: 'The pardoned criminal bears no penalty, but he bears a stigma. He is a criminal and he is known as a criminal, albeit an unpunished one. The justified sinner not only bears no penalty; he is righteous. He is not a man with sin still about him. The effect of Christ's work is to remove sin completely.'[20]

There is nothing incomplete, provisional or temporary about God's verdict. Let me illustrate by way of contrast. In 1941 an American missionary called Bruce Hunt was working among

Koreans in Manchuria when he was captured by the invading Japanese forces. He was eventually brought to trial on a series of obscure charges connected with the Law for the Control of Religions. At the end of the trial the judge pronounced the verdict: 'You are without crime.' Hunt could hardly believe his ears. 'Is this a suspended sentence?' he asked. 'No', the judge replied, 'it is not a suspended sentence. It is a two-year suspended judgement. It means that they have not found you guilty. And if for two years you don't get into trouble, everything will be all right. They have not found you guilty,' he repeated. 'You are without crime.' 'Then why the two-year suspended judgement?' Hunt asked. 'That means', the judge explained, 'that while they have not found you guilty, neither do they declare you not guilty. The judgement one way or another has been left hanging.'[21] There is no such condition attached to God's verdict when he declares someone justified. It is clear, definite and final.

The double death

This chapter has all been about the death of Jesus, but it would be more accurate to speak about the *deaths* of Jesus, because while he was hanging on the cross *he died twice*. We have already established his physical death — the separation of his spirit from his body — but it is very important to notice what the Bible says about his *spiritual* death, the separation of his spirit from God. This is how Mark records it: 'At the sixth hour darkness came over the whole land until the ninth hour. And at the ninth hour Jesus cried out in a loud voice, "*Eloi, Eloi, lama sabachthani?*"[22] — which means, "My God, my God, why have you forsaken me?"' (Mark 15:33-34).

However the sudden darkness was caused, God clearly meant it as a terrifying symbol of the spiritual darkness that descended upon Jesus at that time. In a way that is utterly

beyond our understanding, Jesus sensed that his Father had
turned his back on him, leaving him without any awareness of
his presence. Only hours before, when his closest earthly friends
were on the brink of deserting him, he had been able to say,
'Yet I am not alone, for my Father is with me' (John 16:32).
Now even that assurance was gone. Quite apart from its deeper
meaning, that is remarkable, because God often seems to make
his presence especially real to those who suffer and die for their
faith in him. The way in which Christian martyrs go to their
deaths has produced some of the most powerful and moving
words ever recorded. The great nineteenth-century preacher
C. H. Spurgeon once said that the deaths recorded in *Foxe's
Book of Martyrs* (first published in 1563) were 'all lit up with
the presence of the Lord'.[23] Yet the death of God's sinless Son
was not lit up with the sense of his presence, but darkened by
the sense of his absence.

It is impossible to describe what Jesus went through during
those three hours when 'God made him who had no sin to be
sin for us' (2 Corinthians 5:21) and as a result caused him to
endure the full blast of God's divine anger. What we do know is
that when God poured out his righteous punishment upon him
he was plunged into all the horror and agony that the Bible has
in mind when it speaks about hell. Commenting on this, R. B.
Kuiper wrote, 'That cry was one of hellish agony. When Christ
uttered it, all the waves and billows of the divine wrath against
sin rolled over his head and crushed his soul; he was at the very
bottom of the bottomless pit.'[24] Let me add two other comments. Firstly, Christ's separation from God the Father shows
God's perfect and unchanging justice. God is so unflinching
and unyielding in his holy determination to punish sin and to
banish the sinner from his presence that he did not even make
an exception in the case of his own beloved Son. When Jesus
took the place of sinners he became as accountable for their
sins as if he had been responsible for them. Secondly, his cry of

dereliction shows that *Jesus paid sin's penalty in full.* There was no sleight of hand here, no back-room deal. The separation of Father and Son was actual, spiritual and dreadful, and in experiencing it Jesus met in full the demands of God's holy law. His physical death alone would have achieved little or nothing. At best it would have been a part payment. But by enduring the double death penalty Jesus paid sin's debt in full. In G. Campbell Morgan's words, 'He passed to the uttermost limit of sin's outworking.'[25]

Questions

This has been a long chapter. It had to be if we were not to skate over an event that has been called 'the centre of the world's history'. Of course, there are still unanswered questions. How could one man possibly — or properly — take the place of others and bear their sins? Surely it is immoral of God to punish an innocent third party? How can something done 2,000 years ago affect sins committed by me today? There *are* answers to those questions, *and they all centre around the identity of the one who died.* Who is 'the real Jesus'? We will soon turn our full attention to that question, but before we do so there is one more major event we need to examine.

7.

The man who came back

Jesus died when he was in his early thirties, and if that had been the end of the story this book would never have been written. What forces it into print is the Bible's insistence that *three days later he rose from the dead.*

Needless to say, those eight words trigger off a barrage of questions. What does 'rose from the dead' mean? How can we *know* that he did? What are the implications? Is there a more straightforward explanation for what the Bible seems to say? There are many others: in this chapter we will look for the answers.

Narrative in a nutshell

Shortly after Jesus died, a wealthy follower called Joseph, from the town of Arimathea, got Pontius Pilate's permission to remove the body. After getting help to take it down from the cross, he wrapped it in linen and placed it in his own private tomb, carved out of rock in a nearby garden. At least two women (both called Mary) watched the burial take place. The entrance to the tomb was then covered with a huge stone.

The next day, Jewish religious leaders reminded Pilate that Jesus had prophesied that he would rise from the dead in three days. To prevent his followers removing the body and then claiming that he had done this, Pilate agreed to provide extra security. A detachment of soldiers was posted at the tomb and Pilate's official seal was attached to the stone covering the entrance.

Jesus died at about 3 p.m. on Friday and, as a devout Jew, Joseph ensured that he was buried before the Sabbath began at 6 p.m. But when the two Marys, with another woman called Salome, returned to the garden on Sunday morning, there was no guard, the seal was broken, the stone was rolled away from the entrance — and the body had gone. Suddenly, an angel appeared and told the women not to be afraid, because Jesus had risen from the dead exactly as he had prophesied. They were on their way back into the city to tell the disciples when Jesus himself appeared to them and told them to inform the disciples that he would meet them later. The Gospels and Acts then record eleven separate occasions when Jesus met with individuals or groups of people over the course of the following seven weeks. After a final conversation with some of them near the town of Bethany, 'He left them and was taken up into heaven' (Luke 24:51).

Missing person

So much for the outline, now for the detail. We begin with something over which there can be no argument: on that Sunday morning *the body had gone*. At least five people who visited the site that day confirmed this, and not a single person is known to have denied it. This is remarkable, because within a few weeks Jesus' friends were risking their lives on the streets of Jerusalem by preaching that he had come back to life. Yet if the tomb was not really empty, all the authorities had to do to prove the preachers deluded fools was to invite their hearers to visit the tomb! As the German theologian Paul Althaus says, 'The resurrection proclamation could not have been maintained in Jerusalem for a single day, for a single hour, if the emptiness of the tomb had not been established as a fact for all concerned.'[1]

The empty tomb falls a long way short of proving that Jesus rose from the dead, but preaching that he was alive while his body lay in the grave falls even further short of sanity. The presence of the body would rule out resurrection; the absence of the body at least keeps it on the agenda — and on this issue at least the enemies of Jesus could not deny this vital piece of circumstantial evidence.

Mislaid? Misled?

For 2,000 years, sceptics have been trying to find an alternative explanation to Jesus' resurrection. The writer Kersopp Lake put one ingenious suggestion forward in 1907. His theory was that on that first Sunday morning the three women went to the wrong tomb. They were emotionally disturbed, and in the half-light — Luke tells us that it was 'very early in the morning' (Luke 24:1) — they got their bearings wrong. Mark tells us that when they arrived they were met by 'a young man dressed in a white robe sitting on the right side, and they were alarmed. "Don't be alarmed," he said. "You are looking for Jesus the Nazarene, who was crucified... He is not here. See the place where they laid him"' (Mark 16:5-6). Matthew identifies the 'young man' as 'an angel of the Lord' (Matthew 28:2) — a common exchange of words in the Bible — but Lake suggests that he was just a young man who happened to be in the cemetery at the time. Guessing why they had come, he pointed them to the right tomb, but the women panicked and ran away.

So much for the theory; but it leaks like a sieve. Firstly, is it really likely that the women would have gone to the wrong tomb? Two of them had been present at the burial just thirty-six hours earlier and Mark specifically says that they 'saw where he was laid' (Mark 15:47). The word translated 'saw' is one used of a person 'who looks at a thing with interest and for a purpose, usually indicating the careful observation of details'.[2] Would they really forget what they had seen — *and where they had seen it?*

Secondly, Kersopp Lake wrote, 'It is very doubtful if they were close to the tomb at the moment of burial… It is likely that they were watching at a distance.'[3] But the Bible gives a very different picture and says that the women 'saw the tomb *and how his body was laid in it'* (Luke 23:55). The language is specific and meticulous. How could they have seen all this 'from a distance'? Lake is a long way from Luke!

Thirdly, it is one thing to suggest that three distraught women made a mistake in bad lighting conditions, but this would not account for what happened later in the day. When the women told the disciples, Peter and John ran to the tomb to see for themselves. Did they also go to the wrong one? Some time later, one of the Marys returned. Did she repeat her earlier mistake — in broad daylight and with the benefit of having been re-routed by the young man? The other women also returned. Did they too get it wrong a second time? And did everyone else who may have wanted to check the reports also go to the wrong tomb? Are we really to believe that on that Sunday morning people were dashing all over the cemetery looking for one new grave, and that not one of them could find the right one?

Fourthly, *why did nobody ask Joseph*, the owner of the tomb? Is it conceivable that this prominent citizen would reserve his own private burial place and then forget where it was — especially when he had recently been there to lay to rest the body of a very dear friend?

But the final blow to the theory's credibility is that Lake left out three vital words in the young man's message — *'He has risen!'* (I left them out of the quotation from Mark 16 to accommodate Lake's idea.) Yet there is no justification for this. As Professor Sir Norman Anderson says, Lake's theory 'is based on accepting the beginning and the end of what the young man said, but rejecting the most important part in the middle... This changes the whole meaning; and it seems strange for a scholar to mutilate the record in this way without any textual authority whatever.'⁴ As Lake could put forward his bizarre theory only by tampering with the text, we can safely reject what he says.

Removal or robbery?

Another idea suggests that at some time between Friday evening and Sunday morning the body of Jesus was removed from the tomb. That would obviously explain its absence, but the theory soon runs into difficulties. There could be only four possible 'suspects', and to establish a case against any of them an investigator would want to show that they had both motive and opportunity. Let us see whether they did.

The first suggestion is that the body was stolen by 'a person or persons unknown'. There is not a shred of evidence for this, but what about motive and opportunity? What motive could thieves have had? There had been no elaborate funeral suggesting that the deceased had been wealthy and had his treasures buried with him. Jesus was penniless and the only things in the tomb of any possible commercial value were the linen grave-clothes and about thirty-four kilograms of myrrh and aloes, aromatic spices that had been layered into the grave-clothes 'in accordance with Jewish burial customs' (John 19:40). Yet as we shall see later these were left behind, which would mean that the only thing stolen was a naked corpse. But why would anyone do this? As Professor Anderson says, 'A Jew of that period could scarcely be suspected of stealing bodies on behalf of anatomical research!'⁵

And what opportunity would a thief have had? How could he (or they) have overcome an armed Roman guard?[6] The whole idea is so ridiculous that at least 500 years passed before anybody suggested it — yet it still appeals to some people. The British author Malcolm Muggeridge is a well-known modern example. In his book *Jesus Rediscovered* he writes, 'I even prefer to suppose that some body-snatcher, accustomed to hanging about Golgotha to pick up anything that might be going, heard in his dim-witted way that the King of the Jews was up for execution. "Good!" he thinks: "there are bound to be pickings there." So he waits till the job is done, finds out where the corpse has been laid, drags the stone away and then, making sure no one is watching, decamps with the body. What a disappointment for him! This King of the Jews has no crown, no jewels, no orbs, no sceptre, no ring; he is just a worthless, wasted, broken, naked body. The man contemptuously abandons the body to the vultures, who in their turn leave the bones to whiten in the sun...'[7]

Notice the absence of evidence! The best that Muggeridge can manage is 'I ... prefer to suppose...'; but as elsewhere in the same book he says that the Genesis account of creation is a legend, questions the miraculous virgin conception of Jesus, and considers the doctrine of the Trinity 'perfectly harmless' but 'totally without significance' he is hardly a reliable guide.

The second suggestion is that *the Roman authorities* removed the body. They obviously had the opportunity, and the Roman soldiers would have obeyed orders to remove the body — but why would the authorities give such an order? Pilate was understandably jumpy about the Jesus case, which is why he agreed to post the guard, but surely an armed guard and the governor's seal (tampering with it would have meant death by crucifixion) were sufficient security? What possible advantage could there be in removing the body and placing it under another guard elsewhere? As Pilate's one concern was to get rid of the case (and the sooner the better), repossessing the body would hardly help.

But the theory collapses for another reason. Seven weeks later, when the followers of Jesus began preaching that he had risen from the dead, the Roman authorities could have silenced them at once by producing the body, and if they had done so the whole Christian movement would have been strangled at birth. There can be only one reason for their failure to do so: they had no body to produce.

The next 'suspects' are *the Jewish religious authorities*, who certainly had both opportunity and motive. In spite of national-istic differences, they were obviously working with the Romans in handling the Jesus case. Knowing about Jesus' prophecies that he would rise again after three days, they could have easily proved him wrong by taking the body into their own posses-sion *for four days*. A few words with the Romans about the mutual advantages of squashing a movement that had caused them both so much trouble might just do the trick.

Yet this is all guesswork, with no supporting evidence, and the theory collapses for the same reason as the previous one. When the preaching of the resurrection of Jesus swept through Jerusalem, threatening the religious establishment, *why did the Jews not produce the body?* Instead, they had the preachers arrested, imprisoned, flogged and killed — all totally unneces-sary if they had produced the body. The inference is obvious. In the words of the Scottish theologian Professor Andrew Fairbairn, 'The silence of the Jews is as significant as the speech of the Christians.'[8]

The last 'suspects' are *the disciples of Jesus*, but in the first place it is difficult to see what their motive might have been. Their friend's body had been reverently buried in the tomb of an influential follower who was a leading member of the com-munity. Why should they want to move it elsewhere? They might in theory have done so to prove a false basis for an invented resurrection story, but as we shall see shortly that idea runs into impossible obstacles. As for the opportunity, we can begin not with a theory but with a lie, deliberately invented by the Jewish religious leaders. While on duty at the tomb, the guards had been shaken by a violent earthquake, then stunned by the appearance of an angel who rolled away the huge stone to reveal an empty tomb. When they came out of shock some of the guards rushed into the city to report to the chief priests. Matthew records their reaction: 'When the chief priests had met with the elders and devised a plan, they gave the soldiers a large sum of money, telling them, "You are to say, 'His disciples came during the night and stole him away while we were asleep.' If this report gets to the governor, we will satisfy him and keep you out of trouble." So the soldiers took the money and did as they were instructed' (Matthew 28:12-15).

The priests accepted that the tomb was empty, and it is easy to see why they reacted as they did. If the guards' report got around it would be the ideal platform for claiming that Jesus had risen from the dead — with serious implications for those responsible for killing him. A hurried meeting was called with other members of the Sanhedrin and a face-saving plan cobbled together, but as soon as we ask a few questions it collapses like a house of cards. Would picked Roman guards have been careless enough to fall asleep on duty when (as we know from contemporary Roman military records)[9] the penalty for doing so was execution? Would *every one of them* (a Roman guard had up to sixty men) have done so? How did the disciples manage to get past all the soldiers, break open the seal, roll away the huge stone, and make off with the body without disturbing even one of them? And, if the guards were asleep, *how would they know who stole the body?* Would the disciples have left visiting cards?

The story about the body being snatched while the guard snoozed should be treated with the contempt it deserves; but

what about an alternative version — that the disciples stole the
body while the guards were awake? It is an interesting theory,
but woefully weak. We know that when Jesus was arrested his
followers 'deserted him and fled' (Mark 14:50) and that by the
time he was executed they were reduced to a paralysed rabble.
After the crucifixion, they went into hiding 'with the doors locked
for fear of the Jews' (John 20:19), terrified that they might be
next on the authorities' 'hit list'. Can we imagine this handful of
petrified men suddenly plucking up the courage to tackle an
armed Roman guard and then risking the death penalty by
breaking the governor's official seal — all for the purpose of
taking possession of a body that was already in the safe keeping of one of their friends? If they did so, why is there no record
of their ever being charged with the offences involved?

As if that were not enough to destroy it, the theory that the
disciples stole the body runs up against three other problems.
The first is an *ethical* one. These men had spent three years
under the powerful influence of Jesus' teaching, which had set
moral and ethical standards unequalled before or since. Its effect was reflected in their own teaching later on. James wrote,
'Let your "Yes" be yes, and your "No", no, or you will be condemned' (James 5:12). Peter quoted an Old Testament psalm
and wrote,

> 'Whoever would love life
>   and see good days
> must keep his tongue from evil
>   and his lips from deceitful speech'
>
> (1 Peter 3:10).

John wrote, 'Dear children, let us not love with words or tongue
but with actions and in truth' (1 John 3:18). Would these men
have invented such a pack of lies and made it fundamental to
their own teaching?

The second problem is a *spiritual* one. We are not told that Paul was in Jerusalem at the time of the resurrection, but he did meet Jesus later, and is qualified to speak on behalf of all the apostles. Listing things that would follow if Jesus had not been raised to life, he includes the fact that they would have been 'found to be false witnesses about God, for we have testified about God that he raised Christ from the dead' (1 Corinthians 15:15). Notice the sheer audacity of Paul's argument. The word 'found' has the sense of being detected, or caught out; and the phrase 'testified about God' literally means 'testified against God'. Not only would the apostles be claiming to have been witnesses, they would be claiming to have been witnesses of something they knew to be false. What is more, they would be attributing to God something they knew perfectly well he had not done. But these were men with a passionate concern for God's honour and glory! The idea is sheer fantasy.

The third problem is a *psychological* one. No sooner had they begun to preach that Jesus was alive than the apostles ran headlong into conflict with the religious authorities. They were harassed, arrested, bullied, threatened and flogged. Yet when the Sanhedrin gave them strict instructions to stop preaching they replied, 'We must obey God rather than men!' (Acts 5:29), and carried on preaching as if nothing had happened. Eventually, some of them were executed for doing so, but they would never have stood up to persecution if they had removed the body and buried it elsewhere. They might have risked their lives for something they had imagined, *but not for something they had invented.* Men are sometimes prepared to die for convictions, but not for concoctions! For the disciples to bury the body of Jesus and then risk their lives by preaching that he was alive would have been *psychologically impossible*; in John Stott's words, 'Hypocrites and martyrs are not made of the same stuff.'[10]

So much for the theory that Jesus' body was removed by his friends. We can give it an 'A' for creativity, but nothing for credibility. The whole idea was scornfully dismissed by the brilliant second-century theologian Tertullian, who suggested that perhaps a gardener removed the body to prevent crowds of visitors to the tomb from damaging his vegetables!

Back from the brink

The next theory takes a more radical line and suggests that Jesus never actually died on the cross but merely fainted from exhaustion, trauma and loss of blood then, in the cool of the tomb, revived sufficiently to make his way out, and gave his disciples the impression that he had come back from the dead. This suggestion — sometimes called 'the swoon theory' — was popularized by K. H. G. Venturini in the eighteenth century and revived by Hugh Schonfield in his 1965 publication *The Passover Plot*. In this version, Jesus planned to fake his death and simulate the fulfilment of Old Testament predictions about the Messiah, but he suffered one wound too many. His friends failed to revive him, but before dying he asked them to pass on certain messages to the apostles. The apostles mistook the messenger for Jesus, and as there was no body in the tomb, they assumed that Jesus had come back to life. An even more exotic variation[11] suggests that although Jesus' heart stopped beating while he was on the cross, brain death occurred only after he had revived in the tomb and met his disciples, who later cremated his remains.

But the 'swoon theory' never gets to its feet. The Bible makes it clear that Jesus was officially certified as dead: 'Now it was the day of Preparation, and the next day was to be a special Sabbath. Because the Jews did not want the bodies left on the crosses during the Sabbath, they asked Pilate to have the legs broken and the bodies taken down. The soldiers therefore came and broke the legs of the first man who had been crucified with

Jesus, and then those of the other. But when they came to Jesus and found that he was already dead, they did not break his legs. Instead, one of the soldiers pierced Jesus' side with a spear, bringing a sudden flow of blood and water. The man who saw it has given testimony, and his testimony is true. He knows that he tells the truth, and he testifies so that you also may believe' (John 19:31-35).

As we saw in chapter 3, this was an amazing fulfilment of two Old Testament prophecies about the Messiah — one that none of his bones would be broken and the other that his side would be pierced — but another detail is more relevant to us here. The soldiers were under the governor's orders to break the victims' legs (the usual *coup de grace*) and would not have dared to disobey. But there was no need to do this to Jesus, because they 'found that he was already dead'. We dare not miss the importance of this. A trained execution squad was unlikely to take chances, least of all in the case of a 'trouble-maker' like Jesus, but perhaps to make doubly sure, or as a last vicious gesture, one of the soldiers rammed his spear into Jesus' side, 'bringing a sudden flow of blood and water'.

What was John describing? There are at least two viable explanations. When a dying person's heart stops beating the blood inside the heart chambers clots fairly quickly, then sep-arates into parts, the plasma and the red blood cells. The sol-dier probably stabbed Jesus in the region of the heart and lungs and a large spear wound would produce a mixture of these two substances, something a layman might well describe as 'a sud-den flow of blood and water'. The second explanation is based on the fact that the terrible trauma Jesus suffered before and during the crucifixion would almost certainly have caused a build-up of fluid in the pericardial sac surrounding the heart, as well as enlarging the heart chambers with blood. If the spear had pierced these two organs within ten minutes or so of his death, while the blood was still very fluid, the result would have

been the 'sudden flow of blood and water' described by John.
Whatever the exact pathological explanation, John's words have
an impressive ring of truth about them, and help to confirm the
fact that Jesus was dead. Further confirmation came when
Joseph of Arimathea asked for permission to remove the body.
Mark reports what happened: 'Pilate was surprised to hear that
he was already dead. Summoning the centurion, he asked him
if Jesus had already died. When he learned from the centurion
that it was so, he gave the body to Joseph' (Mark 15:44-45).
Surprised that Jesus had died within a few hours (some victims
hung there for days), Pilate was not prepared to take Joseph's
word for it. He called for an official report from the commanding
officer in charge of the execution squad, and only when he
had this first-hand confirmation did he agree to release the
body.

   We have all the evidence any person could reasonably ask
for accepting that Jesus died on the cross, but let us allow the
swoon theory to run its course. Even before he was crucified,
Jesus had gone through severe physical suffering. He had been
arrested some fifteen hours earlier, and dragged before Jewish
and Roman authorities on five occasions before Pilate eventually pronounced the death sentence at 6 a.m. In all of that time,
he had almost certainly gone without sleep, food or water. A
crude crown of thorns had been thrust on his head, he had
been spat upon, beaten with soldiers' fists and repeatedly
thrashed about the head with a stick. He had also been on the
receiving end of a brutal flogging, in which the victim was tied
in a bent position, exposing his bare back, then lashed with the
Roman scourge, an instrument of leather thongs loaded with
pieces of jagged metal or bone. The scourge tore out chunks of
the victim's flesh, and often caused fatal injuries. After this, Jesus
was led to the place of execution, stripped naked, nailed by his
hands to a wooden cross-beam, hoisted on to a vertical pole,
then nailed through the feet and left to die.

The swoon theory now asks us to accept this kind of scenario: exhausted and traumatized, Jesus lost consciousness while hanging on the cross, but remained alive even after the soldier's spear had ripped open his side. While he was being taken down from the cross, carried to the garden and prepared for burial, nobody noticed the slightest suggestion of breathing, and he was then laid in the grave, apparently lifeless. A stone-cold tomb was hardly an intensive care unit, yet at some time during the next thirty-six hours Jesus came out of a coma (revived by the cool air or the strong-smelling spices?) and like some first-century Houdini wriggled his way out of the tightly wound grave-clothes, layered with a sticky embalming substance. With a baffling recovery of energy he pushed aside the massive rock blocking the entrance to the tomb and overcame the entire Roman guard before going on his way — presumably naked, as the grave-clothes were left behind. Within a few hours, he had made such a rapid recovery that when he met his disciples he persuaded them, not that he had stumbled back from the brink of death, but that he had conquered death and burst through into a new and radiant life.

One has to give the swoon theory full marks for inventiveness, but nothing for integrity. The last sentence of our reconstruction would be enough to reject it out of hand, because it would mean that after a lifetime in which he never committed a single sin, Jesus suddenly became a blatant and blasphemous liar. Everything we know about his character makes that suggestion ridiculous.

The (not quite) empty tomb

We have examined and rejected six major theories which try to account for the events recorded in the Gospels. What of the evidence in favour of the resurrection? We will begin at the tomb. It is often referred to as 'the empty tomb', but that is not strictly true. By that Sunday morning the body had certainly gone, *but the grave-clothes were still there*, and they provide a fascinating piece of evidence. When Peter went into the tomb, 'He saw the strips of linen lying there, as well as the burial cloth that had been around Jesus' head. The cloth was folded up by itself, separate from the linen' (John 20:6-7). Moments later, John confirmed Peter's findings; but why give a detailed description of how grave-clothes were lying when a momentous issue like resurrection from the dead was at stake? Because the first of these things points to the second!

At Eastern burials in those days, the trunk, arms and legs were tightly wrapped in linen cloth, layered with fragrant spices and gummy substances such as myrrh, which would help to bind everything together. In a New Testament example a man called Lazarus had 'his hands and feet wrapped with strips of linen, and a cloth around his face' (John 11:44). Then what exactly did Peter and John see? 'The strips of linen *lying* there.' The word 'lying' seems straightforward, but there is more to the original Greek word than meets the eye, because it is commonly used of something done in an orderly way. But there was something else; the head-cloth was 'folded up by itself, separate from the linen'. One scholar says that 'folded up by itself' means something like 'twirled about itself',[12] and another that it 'aptly describes the rounded shape which the empty napkin still preserved'.[13]

None of this would apply if any one of the theories we examined was true. Why would anyone removing or stealing the body have taken the time and trouble to strip away grave-clothes smothered in a substance which 'glues linen to the body not less firmly than lead'?[14] How could Jesus have done so if he was barely alive? Why would anyone have carefully arranged the grave-clothes before leaving? But what if by some supernatural power Jesus had suddenly been resurrected from the

dead and his new, resurrection body had passed through the
grave-clothes? The linen winding-sheets would have collapsed
under the weight of the spices, while the head-cloth might well
have more or less kept its shape, like 'a crumbled turban with
no head inside it'.[15]

This is exactly what Peter and John saw. Not only had the
body gone, but the grave-clothes had not been touched in the
process; they had simply subsided when the body disappeared.
The effect on John was instantaneous: 'He saw and believed'
(John 20:8). Those four words are more significant than they
seem. We are told that when John reached the tomb he *'looked
in* at the strips of linen lying there but did not go in' (John 20:5),
and the Greek verb *blepo* suggests a superficial glance from
outside the tomb. Then Peter went in and '*saw* the strips of
linen there...', and the Greek verb changes to *theoreo*, which
often means 'the careful perusal of details in the object'.[16] But
when John '*saw* and believed', the Greek verb is *eidon*, a word
which generally refers to 'the mind and thought of him who
sees'.[17] All of this tells us that John saw not only with his eyes,
but with his mind. He realized the significance of those collapsed grave-clothes — 'and *believed*'.

At that moment, John became the first person in the world
to believe that Jesus had risen from the dead, and what convinced him was not merely the absence of the body but the
way in which the grave-clothes were lying. Peter was not so
sure, and went away 'wondering to himself what had happened'
(Luke 24:12), but he soon had even stronger evidence — the
reappearance of Jesus.

The witnesses

By far the most powerful piece of evidence for the resurrection
of Jesus is the Bible's record of his appearances. There are six

independent, written testimonies to this — by Matthew, Mark, Luke, John, Paul and Peter, three of whom are eyewitnesses — and they record eleven separate appearances over a period of forty days. Before going any further, it might be helpful to list these.

- Mark tells us that 'When Jesus rose early on the first day of the week, he appeared first to Mary Magdalene, out of whom he had driven seven demons' (Mark 16:9). John gives more details of the incident and indicates that it took place soon after Peter and John visited the tomb.
- Next, as a group of women were somewhere between the tomb and the city, 'Jesus met them' (Matthew 28:9).
- Later that day, as two disciples were on their way to Emmaus, a village about seven miles from Jerusalem, 'Jesus himself came up and walked along with them' (Luke 24:15).
- After spending some time with him, these two rushed back to Jerusalem to tell the disciples, but before they could get their story out they were told, 'It is true! The Lord has risen and has appeared to Simon' (Luke 24:34).
- 'While they were still talking about this, Jesus himself stood among them and said to them, "Peace be with you"' (Luke 24:36).
- A week later, while they were in the same house, hiding behind locked doors, 'Jesus came and stood among them and said, "Peace be with you!"' (John 20:26).
- John mentions that some time afterwards 'Jesus appeared again to his disciples, by the Sea of Tiberias', that is, the Sea of Galilee (John 21:1).
- Paul tells us that some time during the following weeks, 'He appeared to more than five hundred of the brothers at the same time' (1 Corinthians 15:6).
- Paul also says that 'He appeared to James' (1 Corinthians 15:7).

- Matthew recalls the eleven disciples going to a mountain in Galilee where 'Jesus came to them' (Matthew 28:18).
- Finally, Luke records that after seven weeks, 'He had led them out to the vicinity of Bethany,' where, after giving some last instructions, 'he left them and was taken up into heaven' (Luke 24:50-51).

There are several later incidents — one involving John and the others Paul — in which Jesus revealed himself after his ascension to heaven. Some were 'visions' of one kind or another, but at least one was not. When Paul lists people to whom Jesus appeared bodily, he adds, 'and last of all he appeared to me also...' (1 Corinthians 15:8), and obviously means that his experience was just as real and objective as theirs. A personal encounter with Jesus was a vital qualification for being an apostle, and when people at Corinth questioned Paul's status he had no hesitation in replying, 'Am I not an apostle? Have I not seen Jesus our Lord?' (1 Corinthians 9:1). Writing of these appearances to the apostles, Luke says that Jesus 'showed himself to these men and gave many *convincing proofs* that he was alive' (Acts 1:3). The word 'convincing' has been added by translators to reinforce the word 'proofs', which the ancient Greeks used for 'the strongest proof of which a subject is susceptible'.[18] But even this avalanche of evidence did not convince some people; when Paul preached about the resurrection to an audience of philosophers at Athens, 'Some of them sneered' (Acts 17:32). Since then, the resurrection accounts have faced three major attacks.

The first suggests that the witnesses were lying. The answer to that is the same as the answer to the suggestion that they removed the body from the tomb. What possible motive could they have had? After all, their claim to have met Jesus brought them nothing but trouble. Contrasting his experience as an apostle with those of some of the false teachers of his day, Paul

wrote, 'I have worked much harder, been in prison more frequently, been flogged more severely, and been exposed to death
again and again. Five times I received from the Jews the forty
lashes minus one. Three times I was beaten with rods, once I
was stoned, three times I was shipwrecked, I spent a night and
a day in the open sea, I have been constantly on the move. I
have been in danger from rivers, in danger from bandits, in
danger from my own countrymen, in danger from Gentiles; in
danger in the city, in danger in the country, in danger at sea;
and in danger from false brothers. I have laboured and toiled
and have often gone without sleep; I have known hunger and
thirst and have often gone without food; I have been cold and
naked. Besides everything else, I face daily the pressure of my
concern for all the churches' (2 Corinthians 11:23-28).

Would he deliberately go through all of that (and eventually
be willing to die) for something he knew he had invented? Would
the other apostles have faced lifelong persecution for preaching
that Jesus was alive when they knew perfectly well that his body
was rotting somewhere? Any psychologist would make short
work of that idea! People often lie to get out of trouble, but
never to get into it.

Seeing things?

The second attack suggests that these sightings of Jesus were
nothing more than hallucinations. That explanation is con-
venient, but not convincing, because hallucinations conform to
certain laws, and the resurrection appearances stubbornly fail
to fit the pattern.

Hallucinations are usually associated with people who are
'at least neurotic, if not actually psychotic',[19] but the witnesses
included not only the tearful Mary Magdalene but the gentle
John, the aggressive Peter, fishermen like Andrew and James,

a civil servant like Matthew and a brilliant intellectual like Paul, to say nothing of a stubborn agnostic like Thomas.

Hallucinations usually take place in favourable circumstances and at times when the person concerned is filled with senti- mental feelings or fond memories; but hardly any of these ap- pearances occurred in places where Jesus and the disciples had spent time together. He appeared in a garden, in a home, on a roadside, out in the country, on the seashore and on a hillside — and at many different times of day.

Hallucinations are intensely personal; they arise from an in- dividual's own subconscious ideas; but we are told not just of individuals but of two, three, seven, eleven and on one occa- sion over 500 people claiming to have met the risen Jesus. While speaking to 200 students at a school assembly a friend of mine illustrated the force of this evidence by solemnly producing a pair of scissors and cutting the headmaster's tie in pieces (by prior arrangement!). He then went on to say something like this: 'Imagine that on the way home you meet a friend who is not here this morning and you tell him that you saw the speaker chop up the headmaster's tie at assembly. He would think you were pulling his leg. But supposing three other students came along and told him the same story, and then that tomorrow all thirty students in your class told him they saw it happen. Now imagine that all 200 of you in this hall told him that you had seen exactly the same thing. Surely he would then have no reason for doubting? That is the kind of evidence Paul pro- duces for the fact that Jesus rose from the dead.'

My friend was right. When Paul wrote that Jesus appeared 'to more than five hundred of the brothers at the same time' he added, 'most of whom are still living' (1 Corinthians 15:6). Paul's readers did not have to take his word for it. At least 250 people could be interrogated, and every one of them would have con- firmed the facts. As Dr W. H. Griffith Thomas comments, 'Hal- lucination involving five hundred people at once and repeated several times is unthinkable.'[20]

We can go further, because hallucinations are often the result of wishful thinking. One expert says, 'In order to have an experience like this, one must so intensely *want* to believe that he projects something that really isn't there and attaches reality to his imagination.'[21] There are some people who stubbornly refuse to believe that a dead hero is no longer alive. They are stunned, confused, and irrational, but that was not the case here. As far as the followers of Jesus were concerned, the whole exciting adventure was over and their hero was dead and buried. When the women went to the tomb on that Sunday morning, they did not go to embrace Jesus but to embalm him. When they saw the angel at the empty tomb, 'they were alarmed' (Mark 16:5). When Mary Magdalene told the disciples that she had seen Jesus, 'they did not believe it' (Mark 16:11). When the disciples told Thomas that Jesus had appeared to them, he said, 'Unless I see the nail marks in his hands and put my finger where the nails were, and put my hand into his side, I will not believe it' (John 20:25). Mark records that on one occasion Jesus 'rebuked them for their lack of faith and their stubborn refusal to believe those who had seen him after he had risen' (Mark 16:14). Several weeks later, when many of the followers had become completely convinced, 'some doubted' (Matthew 28:17). This hardly sounds like people jumping to emotionally triggered conclusions! As Leon Morris says, 'The apostles were not men poised on the brink of belief and needing only the shadow of an excuse before launching forth into a proclamation of resurrection. They were utterly sceptical.'[22]

Paul's case is even clearer. His religious training convinced him that Jesus was a blasphemous fake who fell foul of the Old Testament that 'anyone who is hung on a tree is under God's curse' (Deuteronomy 21:23). Convinced that this was the case, Paul began persecuting Jesus' followers, 'arresting both men and women and throwing them into prison' (Acts 22:4). But while he was leading a raiding-party to Damascus, Jesus suddenly appeared to him. Not only was this the last thing he expected, *it was the last thing he wanted*. Paul was no wishful thinker. It took more than a hallucination to change a persecutor into a preacher!

We have examined only some of the conditions normally required for hallucination. There are others, but the Gospel narratives fit none of them, and a thorough examination of the facts leads a medical expert like Professor A. Rendle Short to conclude that 'The resurrection appearances break every known law of visions.'[23] Dr J. Gresham Machen adds the wry comment that had the witnesses been hallucinating, it would mean that 'if there had been a good neurologist for Peter and the others to consult, there would never have been a Christian church'![24]

Ghost story?

One variation of the 'hallucination theory' is the suggestion that what the disciples saw was some kind of spirit or ghost. The German writer Karl Theodor Keim popularized this in the nineteenth century, but it is totally at odds with the straightforward wording of Scripture. When he appeared to two disciples on the road to Emmaus, he went into the house with them, 'took bread, gave thanks, broke it and began to give it to them' (Luke 24:30). This alone is sufficient to put paid to Keim's conjecture (ghosts are not in the habit of passing food around!) but the most telling evidence against it came when the two travellers reported to other disciples in Jerusalem: 'While they were still talking about this, Jesus himself stood among them and said to them, "Peace be with you." They were startled and frightened, thinking they saw a ghost. He said to them, "Why are you troubled, and why do doubts rise in your minds? Look at my hands and my feet. It is I myself! Touch me and see; a ghost does not have flesh and bones, as you see I have." When he had said this, he showed them his hands and feet. And while they still did not believe it because of joy and amazement, he asked them, "Do you have anything here to eat?" They gave him a piece of broiled fish, and he took it and ate it in their presence' (Luke 24:36-43). Jesus never denied the existence of disembodied spirits, but he made it crystal clear that he was not one. Instead, he appealed to their senses — sight, hearing and touch — and even ate a piece of fish to clinch the point. Later, on the seashore at Galilee, Jesus invited seven of them to 'Come and have breakfast' (John 21:12). This made such a powerful impression upon Peter that in one of his sermons he specifically speaks of the apostles as those 'who ate and drank with him after he rose from the dead' (Acts 10:41). Finally, there was the incident with the sceptical Thomas, who said that he would not believe unless he touched the wounds made in Jesus' body by the nails and spear. Jesus challenged his scepticism head-on: 'Put your finger here; see my hands. Reach out your hand and put it into my side. Stop doubting and believe' (John 20:27).

All of this proves that when Jesus rose from the dead he had a *physical* body, yet one without the usual limitations. He left the grave-clothes without disturbing them and could appear and disappear at will. (This could explain why there were times when those who met him did not recognize him immediately, and why they always did so eventually.) It makes his resurrection unique. The Bible records a number of people who were restored to life — at least three of them by Jesus — but each one of them eventually died again. They were resuscitated rather than resurrected, which is exactly why Jesus is called 'the *first* to rise from the dead' (Acts 26:23). What is more, the Bible says that 'He cannot die again; death no longer has mastery over him. The death he died, he died to sin once for all; but the life he lives, he lives to God' (Romans 6:9-10). As Martyn Lloyd-Jones put it, 'His raising from the dead is a proclamation that death is conquered and vanquished by him, and that he will never die again.'[25] In his resurrection, Jesus was taken out of the sphere in which death operates and into a dimension of life beyond human experience and explanation.

Ring of truth

So much for attempts to explain away the Bible's record that Jesus was seen alive by hundreds of people after his death and burial. The evidence remains impressively intact, and we can add three unexpected credentials which give the Gospel narratives an unmistakable ring of truth.

Firstly, there is no description of the resurrection itself. Surely that is significant? If the apostles had cooked up the story, they would hardly have been able to resist the temptation to include a dramatic eyewitness account of the tomb bursting open and Jesus striding out in shining power. Instead there is nothing; nobody saw it happen. No creative novelist would settle for that!

Secondly, we are told that the first time Jesus appeared it was to a woman, yet in those days a woman's testimony was considered almost worthless. This may partly explain why, when Mary and the other women reported to the apostles, 'They did not believe the women, because their words seemed to them like nonsense' (Luke 24:11). It certainly explains why the second-century philosopher Celsus ridiculed the resurrection as something based on the experiences of a 'hysterical female'.[26] If the apostles had invented the story, they would hardly have made the basic blunder of leaning so heavily on the testimony of distressed women.

Thirdly, it is very difficult to fit the resurrection narratives into a consistent pattern. Details vary, and it is impossible to put the stories into chronological order. This may seem like a weakness, but is exactly the opposite. Had the apostles concocted the story they would have ensured that all the accounts agreed in every detail. Instead, although they are unanimous in saying that the grave was empty and that Jesus was seen alive, the accounts differ in detail. This is a strong point in their favour. I regularly read two daily national newspapers, and when two or more reports of an event differ in detail, I never jump to the conclusion that the event never took place. In a court of law, several witnesses may each give truthful accounts of an incident as they saw it, yet their testimonies may vary considerably without contradicting the essential truth of what happened. In this case the variations do not contradict each other on any point of detail. Instead, they are all woven around the central core of events and give us every reason for believing that the witnesses' accounts are fact, not fiction. They have a ring of truth about them.

New lives for old

As we saw earlier, the arrest and death of Jesus left his followers a dejected and paralysed rabble, terrified that their turn might be next. Yet seven weeks later they came out of hiding, took to the streets, and risked their lives by preaching that Jesus was alive. Even more remarkably, their chief spokesman was Peter, who had not only deserted Jesus when the chips were down, but had denied that he even knew him. Yet when he and John were arrested and brought before the Sanhedrin for preaching the resurrection, Peter never retracted a word, and his accusers were amazed at 'the *courage* of Peter and John' (Acts 4:13). Cowardice to courage is a tremendous transformation — one scholar calls it 'almost unbelievable in its sudden completeness'[27] — and the Gospels give only one explanation.

The same change came over all the apostles. They threw off their inhibitions and fears and staked their lives on one thing:

Jesus was alive. Nothing — neither ridicule, persecution, imprisonment nor the threat of execution — could stop them. They were transformed, radiant and irresistible. Fear had given way to faith, despair to delight and paralysis to power. Norman Anderson is not exaggerating when he says, 'Far and away the strongest circumstantial evidence for the resurrection ... can be found in the startling change in the apostles.'[28]

The mustard-seed movement

The next piece of circumstantial evidence for the resurrection is linked to the last, because humanly speaking the apostles were the founders of a movement which gave a dynamic new expression to true faith in God. It got off to an electrifying start: on the very first day of public preaching 'three thousand were added to their number' (Acts 2:41). Soon 'the number of men grew to about five thousand' (Acts 4:4). Within a few years, their enemies accused Paul and his fellow preachers of having 'caused trouble all over the world' (Acts 17:6). That may have been a panicky exaggeration, but by the early part of the fourth century Christianity had spread so far and penetrated society so deeply that it was recognized as the official religion of the same Roman Empire that had tried to stamp it out by killing Jesus. Some 2,000 years later the Christian church is the largest religious movement in the world. In one of his parables about the kingdom of God, Jesus said, 'It is like a mustard seed, which is the smallest seed you plant in the ground. Yet when planted, it grows and becomes the largest of all garden plants...' (Mark 4:31-32). It is difficult to miss the connection!

What started it all? What persuaded its founders to break away from their ancient religious moorings and launch a totally new movement? It was not a new approach that overturned the Old Testament's moral teaching. Jesus made that very clear:

'Do not think that I have come to abolish the Law or the
Prophets; I have not come to abolish them but to fulfil them'
(Matthew 5:17). Time and again he endorsed Old Testament
teaching, and never once contradicted it. In Michael Green's
words, 'It was certainly not the Sermon on the Mount that produced Christianity.'[29] Nor was it an original slant on social issues.
There was nothing new in his manifesto about the redistribution
of wealth, the emancipation of slaves or the revision of the
political system.

There was just one thing that triggered off this new move-
ment and fuelled its dynamic growth — *the resurrection of Jesus*.
Its message was not an ethic, but an event; not a philosophy,
but a fact. In the choice of an apostle to replace the dead traitor
Judas Iscariot, the qualifications included not only being with
Jesus during the three years of his public ministry, but also being
'a witness with us of *his resurrection*' (Acts 1:22). The climax of
Peter's first sermon was his statement that '*God has raised this
Jesus to life*' (Acts 2:32). When crowds of people were aston-
ished that he had healed a cripple, Peter told them that the
miracle had been performed by the power of Jesus, whom 'God
raised ... *from the dead*' (Acts 3:15). When Peter and John
were dragged before the Sanhedrin, it was because they were
'teaching the people and proclaiming in Jesus *the resurrection
of the dead*' (Acts 4:2). When questioned about their miraculous power, they replied, 'It is by the name of Jesus Christ of
Nazareth, whom you crucified but *whom God raised from the
dead*, that this man stands before you [completely] healed' (Acts
4:10). Some time later, when Peter preached in Caesarea to a
Roman army officer and his family and friends, his sermon
centred around Jesus, and focused on the same fact: '*God raised
him from the dead* on the third day and caused him to be seen'
(Acts 10:40). Wherever he went, Paul's preaching had exactly
the same emphasis. At Pisidian Antioch he had no sooner mentioned the death of Jesus than he added, 'But *God raised him*

from the dead' (Acts 13:30). To the city fathers in Athens he spoke of God *'raising him from the dead'* (Acts 17:31). He told believers in Corinth that it was the linchpin of his message: 'For what I received I passed on to you as of first importance: that Christ died for our sins according to the Scriptures, that he was buried, that *he was raised on the third day* according to the Scriptures, and that he appeared to Peter, and then to the Twelve' (1 Corinthians 15:3-5). No wonder he told them that 'If Christ has not been raised, our preaching is useless...' (1 Corinthians 15:14) — a word meaning 'empty, worthless'.

The resurrection of Jesus dominates New Testament preaching, and has led to this comment by the historian Kenneth Scott Latourette: 'It was the conviction of the resurrection of Jesus which lifted his followers out of the despair into which his death had cast them and which led to the perpetuation of the movement begun by him. But for their profound belief that the crucified had risen from the dead and that they had seen him and talked with him, the death of Jesus and even Jesus himself would probably have been all but forgotten.'[30]

Sabbath, Sunday and symbols

The resurrection of Jesus also produced revolutionary changes in religious customs. For well over 1,000 years, Jews had observed the Sabbath (Saturday) as a day of rest and worship in obedience to the fourth of the Ten Commandments. Yet almost immediately these first Christians (almost all devout Jews) began to meet for worship on 'the first day of the week' (Acts 20:7) — that is, Sunday — and eventually they abandoned the old Sabbath altogether. They did so to commemorate the day on which Jesus rose from the dead, and no other movement in history has succeeded in making such a change. The more you think about it, the more amazing it becomes. As William Milligan says,

'It was this fact [the resurrection of Jesus] that made the difference, and a more powerful testimony to men's conviction of the truth of the event, within a week after it is said to have happened, it would be impossible to produce.'[31]

My native island of Guernsey, off the north-west coast of France, was invaded by the Germans during World War II and remained under enemy occupation for several years. But on 9 May 1945 it was liberated by the British forces, and on that date each year we celebrate Liberation Day, as a joyful reminder of that event. Try telling Guernseymen that liberation never took place, and that we are celebrating a figment of our imagination!

The resurrection also lies behind the two Christian sacraments of baptism and Holy Communion. For centuries, Jews had practised circumcision as a sign of entry into God's family. Yet the early church replaced it with baptism, and Paul explains why: 'We were therefore buried with him through baptism into death in order that, just as Christ was raised from the dead through the glory of the Father, we too may live a new life' (Romans 6:4). Christian baptism makes no sense unless Jesus rose from the dead.

The same is true of Holy Communion (sometimes known as the Lord's Supper or the Breaking of Bread) which took the place of the centuries-old Passover feast. Jesus instituted the change at a final Passover meal with his disciples, saying that from then on the bread and wine would symbolize his body and blood and were to be taken 'in remembrance of me' (Luke 22:19). After the resurrection, the members of the early church obeyed his instructions 'with glad and sincere hearts, praising God...' (Acts 2:46-47). The word translated 'glad' conveys the idea of 'jubilant exultation'.[32] It was not a morbid memorial meal for a dead friend, but an expression of their fellowship with one who was alive. In the same way that Christians call the day on which Jesus died Good Friday (because of all that

he accomplished in his death) so they 'celebrate' Holy Communion — a word that makes sense only if Jesus rose from the
dead and is 'alive for ever and ever!' (Revelation 1:18).

The church's origin, preaching, power, growth, endurance
and influence all point to one stupendous event: Jesus rose
from the dead. As someone has rightly said, 'The Christian
church has resurrection written all over it.'[33]

The verdict

The philosopher Professor C. E. M. Joad, an original member
of BBC Radio's famous Brains Trust, was once asked, 'If you
could ask one question and be sure of getting the right answer,
what would it be?' His reply was this: 'Did Jesus Christ rise
from the dead?' This chapter has shown the importance of that
question and the clarity of the Bible's answer to it.

Over the last 2,000 years millions of people have come to
accept that evidence, with all its consequences. In the nineteen-
twenties journalist Frank Morison accepted the popular idea
that the Gospels were basically unreliable, not least because he
thought science had disproved miracles. However, he was very
impressed with the character of Jesus, and decided to write a
book called Jesus, the Last Phase, which would concentrate on
the last week of his earthly life and reveal something of his true
character. As he sifted through the evidence for himself it brought
about what he called 'a revolution in my thought'.[34] Jesus, the
Last Phase 'was left high and dry, like those Thames barges,
when the great river goes out to meet the incoming sea'.[35] Instead, Morison wrote a book entitled Who Moved the Stone? in
which he argued powerfully for the truth of the resurrection story.

In many cases even renowned legal experts have completely
revised their previous judgements. In the early part of the

eighteenth century two brilliant young men, Gilbert West and
Lord Lyttleton, went to Oxford University. They were strongly
opposed to Christianity and at the end of one academic year
set each other a summer holiday assignment which they believed would reinforce their views: Lyttleton would prove that
Paul never became a Christian, and West that Jesus never rose
from the dead. When they met again in the autumn to compare notes they both had to admit that they had been forced to
opposite conclusions: Paul *had* become a Christian and Jesus
did rise from the dead. West's findings were later published in
1747 under the title *Observations on the History and Evidence
of the Resurrection of Jesus Christ.*

Dr Simon Greenleaf, the outstanding Harvard professor who
died in 1853 and whose work *A Treatise on the Law of Evidence* was considered the greatest work of its kind, became
completely convinced that the apostles were telling the truth. In
Greenleaf's words, 'It was … impossible that they could have
persisted in affirming the truths they have narrated, had not
Jesus actually risen from the dead, and had they not known
this fact as certainly as they knew any other fact.'[36]

Lord Lyndhurst was one of the greatest minds in British legal
history, eventually serving as High Steward of Cambridge University. In a document found among his private papers after his
death in 1863 he delivered this powerful verdict: 'I know pretty
well what evidence is; and I tell you, such evidence as that for
the resurrection has never broken down yet.'[37]

Lord Darling, a former Chief Justice of England, said that
'There exists such overwhelming evidence, positive and nega-
tive, factual and circumstantial, that no intelligent jury in the
world could fail to bring in a verdict that the resurrection story
is true.'[38]

Sir Edward Clarke, K.C., wrote, 'As a lawyer I have made a
prolonged study for the events of the first Easter Day. To me

the evidence is conclusive, and over and over again in the High Court I have secured the verdict on evidence not nearly so compelling.'[39]

Ultimately, accepting that Jesus rose from the dead is a matter of faith, but it is not a leap in the dark. It is based on an unshakeable mass of persuasive evidence.

Postscript

Our investigation into the resurrection is nearly complete, but we need to ask one last question: *whose power brought it about?* The Bible's answer is in two parts, one surprising and the other not so. Before we consider these, notice how the Bible emphasizes the tremendous power involved in bringing about such a miracle. When Paul writes about God's power at work in the lives of his people, he compares it to 'the working of his mighty strength, which he exerted in Christ when he raised him from the dead...' (Ephesians 1:19-20). But why not use some other illustration, such as God's power in creation, or in upholding the universe, or in his dramatic interventions in human history, both in delivering his people and in destroying their enemies? Why choose the resurrection? Because in raising Jesus from the dead, *man's greatest enemy was overcome.*

Death is one of the greatest facts of life. Nobody, however powerful, gifted, wealthy or influential, can prevent death's coming or resist its power. As the sixteenth-century preacher William Gurnall wrote, 'We can as soon run from ourselves as run from death.' But in the resurrection of Jesus death was overcome. In a stupendous display of supernatural power he 'has destroyed death and has brought life and immortality to light through the gospel' (2 Timothy 1:10). In C. S. Lewis's words, 'He has forced open a door that had been locked since the death of the first man. He has met, fought and beaten the King of Death. Everything is different because he has done so.'[40]

But by whose power? The unsurprising part of the Bible's answer is that it was by the power of God. Peter preached that 'God raised him from the dead' (Acts 2:24) and that '*The God of our fathers* raised Jesus from the dead' (Acts 5:30). This is exactly what we would expect. Yet the 'surprising' news is that Jesus rose from the dead *by his own power*. When he threw the swindlers out of the temple at Jerusalem and the Jews demanded a miraculous sign from him to prove his authority to do such a thing, Jesus answered them, "Destroy this temple, and I will raise it again in three days." The Jews replied, "It has taken forty-six years to build this temple, and you are going to raise it in three days?" But the temple he had spoken of was his body. After he was raised from the dead, his disciples recalled what he had said. Then they believed the Scripture and the words that Jesus had spoken' (John 2:19-22). Jesus forecast his resurrection several times, and in doing so put his own reputation on the line; if he had not risen from the dead he would at best have been a self-deceived prophet and at worst a deliberate liar. Now he goes further and says that this amazing miracle (a 'sign' infinitely greater than the one they thought he meant) would be one that he would himself perform. As if that were not enough, he also announced its exact timing, and later proved to be right on schedule!

Nothing we have discovered about Jesus so far is more amazing than this. Here is a man in his early thirties telling people that even if they killed him he would come back to life three days later, *and do so by his own power*. Later he said, 'No one takes [my life] from me, but I lay it down of my own accord. I have authority to lay it down and authority to take it up again' (John 10:18). Just as no power on earth could kill him as long as he chose to stay alive, so no power could prevent him pushing death aside and coming back to life whenever he chose to do so. A few mentally unhinged people in history may have made similar claims, but none of them proved to be telling the truth. Jesus did — *and the explanation lies in his identity. Who is the real Jesus?*

8.

The man who was more

At this point I have a confession to make: I have been withholding important information!

We began our search for 'the real Jesus' by confirming his true existence in history. Then, using the Bible as a database, we uncovered layer after layer of astonishing truth about him. We found that he fulfilled all the Old Testament prophecies about the Messiah and the Son of God, was born of a virgin, lived a sinless life, died to bear the sins of others, rose again from the dead and is eternally alive. Yet even with all this amazing data about his history, we are still left with our fundamental question about his identity: *who is the real Jesus?*

In the musical *Jesus Christ Superstar*, Mary Magdalene sings, 'He's a man, he's just a man,' but that sounds pretty foolish when put alongside the facts. As we have seen (particularly in chapter 5) Jesus certainly *was* a man, but nobody who was 'just a man' could possibly live as he lived or die as he died — let alone rise from the dead. But what, or who is he? Those questions bring us face to face with the main thing the Bible teaches about him — and the vitally important information I have been withholding: Jesus *is* God.

This is not an eccentric interpretation of an obscure statement tucked away in a tiny corner of the Bible; it is the one massive message that glues the whole of Scripture together. As C. S. Lewis wrote, 'The doctrine of Christ's divinity seems to me not something stuck on which you can unstick, but something that peeps out at every point, so that you would have to un-ravel the whole web to get rid of it.'[1] Thousands of books have been written on the subject; somehow, we must try to tackle the essential facts in this one chapter.

Identity claim

What did Jesus himself have to say on the subject? A great deal! Although he could never be accused of conceit he often talked about himself, and particularly about his identity. We saw earlier that he claimed to be God's promised Messiah and the Son of God, enjoying an intimate and eternal relationship with his heavenly Father; but did he ever claim to be God? Yes he did. Although there is no record of his using the phrase, 'I am God', he often made the same stupendous claim using other words.

When Jesus healed a man who had been paralysed for thirty-eight years, sticklers for legalistic detail complained that because he did so on the Sabbath he was breaking the law. Jesus answered the charge by saying, 'My Father is always at his work to this very day, and I, too, am working' (John 5:17). That seems straightforward enough, but it is far from it. Firstly, Jesus was saying that he was not bound by Jewish interpretation of the Sabbath law. God was 'always at his work', providing for and looking after his creation. Secondly, by adding, 'and I, too, am working' he meant 'I am working in the same way that God is working. We are in tandem. Whatever he is doing, I am doing; whatever I am doing, he is doing. He is not bound by your understanding of Sabbath law, *and neither am I.*' That did it! 'For this reason the Jews tried all the harder to kill him; not only was he breaking the Sabbath, but he was even calling God his own Father, *making himself equal with God*' (John 5:18). These Jews understood exactly what Jesus meant, *and he did nothing to correct their interpretation.*

A little later, when the name of the Old Testament patriarch Abraham came up in discussion, Jesus said, 'Your father Abraham rejoiced at the thought of seeing my day; he saw it and was glad.' His opponents snapped back: '"You are not yet fifty years old," the Jews said to him, "and you have seen Abraham!"' Jesus' reply shook them rigid: 'I tell you the truth, before Abraham was born, I am!' (John 8:56-58). What on earth did he mean? One suggestion is that he was claiming to have been born before Abraham, and therefore to be over 2,000 years old (but if so he must have been wearing rather well, as the Jews thought he was under fifty!). Others have suggested that he was merely claiming to have existed before time began, perhaps as an angel or some other being created by God. But neither of these ideas fits the context, or the answer that Jesus gave. The Jews had not asked how old Jesus was, but 'Are you *greater* than our father Abraham?' (John 8:53). The issue was not his age but his identity, and in his reply Jesus did not say, 'Before Abraham was born, I was born,' nor even, 'Before Abraham was born, I was,' but 'Before Abraham was born, *I am*!' What made his words so stunning was that 'I AM' was one of the names by which God had revealed himself in the Old Testament. When giving Moses certain instructions for his people, God said, 'This is what you are to say to the Israelites: "I AM has sent me to you"' (Exodus 3:14). 'I AM' is a title which infers absolute, timeless self-existence, things that can only be true of God. *Yet Jesus calmly used it about himself.* That could only mean one thing: he was claiming to be God. J. C. Ryle says, 'All attempts to evade this explanation appear to me to be so preposterous that it is a waste of time to notice them.'[2] Claiming to be 2,000 years old, or an angel, would be nothing more than eccentric, but claiming to be God was a capital offence, and the Jews immediately 'picked up stones to stone him' (John 8:59). They knew exactly what he was claiming.

The third incident took place when Jesus ended a teaching session by saying, 'I and the Father are one' (John 10:30). The

word 'one' is not masculine, but neuter, which means that Jesus
was not claiming to be one in person with God but one in substance and essence. What followed tells us exactly what he
meant: 'Again the Jews picked up stones to stone him, but Jesus
said to them, "I have shown you many great miracles from the
Father. For which of these do you stone me?" "We are not
stoning you for any of these," replied the Jews, "but for blasphemy, because you, a mere man, *claim to be God*"' (John
10:31-33).

The next claim was made when one of his disciples asked
for concrete evidence on which to build their faith: 'Lord, show
us the Father and that will be enough for us' (John 14:8). The
disciples were not philosophers or theologians, but ordinary
down-to-earth people, for whom seeing believed. Jesus met
the challenge head-on: 'Don't you know me, Philip, even after
I have been among you such a long time? Anyone who has
seen me has seen the Father' (John 14:9). Jesus did not mean
that he *was* the Father, but that anyone who had seen him had
seen, in human form, as much of the Father as it was humanly
possible to see. Centuries before, God had told Moses that 'No
one may see me and live' (Exodus 33:20): now Jesus was saying that in himself he revealed all of God's character and nature that it was possible and necessary for a human being to
see and know. In other words, he was claiming to be God.

Then, a few hours before his death, Jesus prayed, 'And now,
Father, glorify me in your presence with the glory I had with
you before the world began' (John 17:5). He was clearly claiming that this shared glory was not given to him at some time in
the past but something he possessed eternally 'before the world
began'. Either this is blasphemous nonsense or Jesus is
addressing God on equal terms. It is surely not difficult to decide
which is the case?

Shortly afterwards, Jesus was with his disciples in the Garden of Gethsemane when a squad of soldiers (tipped off by

Judas Iscariot) came to arrest him. 'Jesus, knowing all that was
going to happen to him, went out and asked them, "Who is it
you want?" "Jesus of Nazareth," they replied. "I am he," Jesus
said. (And Judas the traitor was standing there with them.) When
Jesus said, "I am he," they drew back and fell to the ground'
(John 18:4-6). What an amazing reaction! Jesus was emotionally exhausted, unarmed, and offering no resistance, yet one
short sentence (just two words in the language he used) and a
whole detachment of armed troops staggered backwards and
clattered to the ground. On that performance, they were hardly
commando material! Then why did they keel over? The explanation lies in the phrase Jesus used. Translators have added the
word 'he' to round out the sentence, but what Jesus actually
said was simply 'I am' (the divine title we noticed earlier), and
the majesty and glory of those words and the way they were
spoken swept the soldiers to the ground in a spectacular dem-
onstration of the presence and power of God.

In other words...

We have looked at six of Jesus' direct claims to deity, but many
indirect comments pointed in the same direction.

For example, he made astonishing claims about his teaching. He endorsed the divine authority of the Old Testament by
saying, 'I tell you the truth, until heaven and earth disappear,
not the smallest letter, not the least stroke of a pen, will by any
means disappear from the Law until everything is accomplished'
(Matthew 5:18), but said the same thing about his own teaching:
'Heaven and earth will pass away, but my words will never
pass away' (Matthew 24:35). He repeatedly corrected false
interpretations of Old Testament principles with statements of
his own, introduced with the phrase, 'But I tell you...' (Matthew 5:22,28,32,34,39,44). The inference was obvious: his

teaching had the same authority as the written Word of God. As one scholar puts it, 'The claims that he made for the authority of his teaching were not simply the claims of a prophet of God to speak the words of God. His words were God's words, because he was God.'[3]

He also made a succession of staggering statements about his ability to meet the spiritual needs of others. Here are some of them: 'I am the bread of life. He who comes to me will never go hungry, and he who believes in me will never be thirsty' (John 6:35); 'I am the light of the world. Whoever follows me will never walk in darkness, but will have the light of life' (John 8:12); 'I am the resurrection and the life. He who believes in me will live, even though he dies; and whoever lives and believes in me will never die' (John 11:25-26); 'I am the way and the truth and the life. No one comes to the Father except through me' (John 14:6). In these statements Jesus said that he alone could meet every individual's need for forgiveness, moral direction, spiritual security and inner peace, and bring him or her into a living and eternal relationship with God. It is difficult to imagine anyone in his right mind making even one of those claims about himself *unless he was God*.

But Jesus went even further. He said that he would be directly involved in all the major events surrounding the end of the world. Shortly before his death he told his disciples that he was going to heaven to prepare a place for them, then added the promise: 'I will come back and take you to be with me that you also may be where I am' (John 14:3). (This is sometimes called the Second Coming of Christ and is mentioned over 300 times in the New Testament.) As the Son of Man he would summon all mankind to the day of divine judgement, and when he did so, 'All who are in their graves will hear his voice and come out — those who have done good will rise to live, and those who have done evil will rise to be condemned' (John 5:28-29). Finally, he himself would be responsible for dispensing eternal judgement, and would 'separate the people one from another as a shepherd separates the sheep from the goats' (Matthew 25:32). Who else but God could properly make statements like these?

At other times Jesus claimed that men's reaction to him was an indication of their reaction to God. On one occasion he told faithless Jews, 'When a man believes in me, he does not believe in me only, but in the one who sent me. When he looks at me, he sees the one who sent me' (John 12:44-45). One day he took a child in his arms and said, 'Whoever welcomes one of these little children in my name welcomes me; and whoever welcomes me does not welcome me but the one who sent me' (Mark 9:37). At another point he said, 'He who does not honour the Son does not honour the Father, who sent him' (John 5:23). In the same vein he told his followers, 'He who hates me hates my Father as well' (John 15:23). What other religious leader could quietly and persistently link himself with God in this way? Montgomery Boice is hardly exaggerating when he says, 'Practically everything Jesus said was an indirect claim to divinity.'[4]

Miracle man

If his teaching was breathtaking, so were his dramatized claims, in other words, his miracles. We read of him healing the blind, the deaf, the dumb, the lame, those with leprosy and the paralysed — in fact, curing 'every disease and sickness' (Matthew 9:35). His miracles also included casting out evil spirits and healing 'all who were under the power of the devil' (Acts 10:38). He brought at least three dead people back to life. He fed over 5,000 people with five loaves and two fish, and 'the disciples picked up twelve basketfuls of broken pieces that were left over' (Matthew 14:20). When a sudden storm swept over the disciples' boat and threatened to drown them, 'he got up and

rebuked the winds and the waves, and it was completely calm'
(Matthew 8:26).

It is sometimes argued that even these miracles are not proof
that Jesus is divine, because other people in the Bible performed
miracles, and three of them (Elijah in the Old Testament and
Peter and Paul in the New) each raised a dead person to life;
but two things about the miracles of Jesus set them apart from
the rest. Firstly, the sheer volume of them. Old Testament miracles are pretty thin on the ground, but Jesus unleashed an
avalanche of miraculous power and may have performed more
miracles in one day than were performed in all the centuries of
Old Testament history. John ends his Gospel by saying, 'Jesus
did many other things as well. If every one of them were written down, I suppose that even the whole world would not have
room for the books that would be written' (John 21:25).

Secondly, Jesus performed his miracles with the same authority that marked his teaching. The Bible often calls them
'miraculous signs' (John 2:11), meaning that they were not an
end in themselves but pointers to Jesus' identity. On one of the
occasions when the Jews threatened to stone him to death for
claiming to be God, Jesus cited his miracles as proof of his
claim: 'Do not believe me unless I do what my Father does. But
if I do it, even though you do not believe me, believe the miracles, that you may know and understand that the Father is in
me, and I in the Father' (John 10:37-38). As one scholar comments, 'The miracles of Jesus ... are not merely ... signs that
the kingdom of God is at hand, but also clear indications that
he by whom the signs are wrought is the Son of God and equal
to God himself.'[5]

The nineteenth-century French artist Paul Gustave Doré lost
his passport while in a foreign country. At the next international
border he explained his problem to an immigration official and
assured him that he was Doré, the well-known painter. The
official handed him a piece of paper and a pencil and said,

'Prove it!' Within a few minutes Doré produced such a brilliant sketch that the official was convinced that he was exactly who he claimed to be. The miracles of Jesus are even clearer proof of an infinitely greater claim.

Eloquent silence

Another way in which Jesus emphasized his claim to be God was by doing nothing! When finally convinced that Jesus had risen from the dead, Thomas, one of his followers, cried out, 'My Lord and my God!' (John 20:28). Yet to worship anyone but God is idolatry, and for anyone but God to accept worship is blasphemy. When the Roman centurion Cornelius met Peter and made as if to worship him, Peter told him, 'Stand up, I am only a man myself' (Acts 10:26). When Paul healed a cripple at Lystra the people thought that he and Barnabas were pagan gods in human form and wanted to offer sacrifices to them, but when the apostles realized what was happening they rushed out into the crowd shouting, 'Men, why are you doing this? We too are only men, human like you' (Acts 14:14-15). Yet when Thomas called him 'My Lord and my God!', Jesus never corrected him; his silence speaks volumes.

Name above all names

Another powerful piece of evidence is the way in which, as some researchers have said, 'Scripture ascribes to Jesus *every* major name, attribute and title of God.'[6] Because many of these instances will emerge later we will concentrate at this point on just one — the greatest of all.

In Old Testament times God's people shied away from making direct references to him by name. They were so reluctant to

spell out his sacred name, Yahweh, that they shortened it to
four consonants, YHWH, and even in that coded form it could
not be used indiscriminately. The Jewish writer Philo, a contemporary of Jesus, said, 'The four letters may be mentioned
or heard only by holy men whose ears and tongues are purified
by wisdom, and by no others in any place whatsoever.'[7] Other
Hebrew words for God included 'adonay' and 'elohim', and in
the twelfth century it was a combination of the consonants
YHWH and the vowels from these two words that produced
the word 'Jehovah' which is sometimes used today.

When the Old Testament was first translated from Hebrew
to Greek, the word most commonly chosen to translate YHWH
and 'adonay' was kyrie, which our English versions almost always render as 'Lord'. The same word, kyrios, was also used
in other ways. Sometimes it was no more than a polite form of
address: Greek visitors to Jerusalem once said to Philip, 'Sir
[kyrie], we would like to see Jesus' (John 12:21). At other times
it was used to denote ownership or authority: Jesus told a parable in which a leading character was 'the owner [kyrios] of the
vineyard' (Matthew 20:8). But in well over 6,000 cases the word
kyrios (Lord) is used as a translation or synonym of one or
other of the major Old Testament words for God, and is meant
to imply that 'the Lord' is the almighty Creator and Sustainer of
the universe to whom all men owe unqualified worship and
obedience.

Yet New Testament writers constantly quote Old Testament
statements about 'the Lord' and apply them to Jesus. Isaiah
called God's people to prepare for a later prophet who would
be 'a voice of one calling: "In the desert prepare the way for the
LORD"' (Isaiah 40:3); centuries later, when John the Baptist announced himself as 'the voice of one calling in the desert, "Make
straight the way for the Lord"' (John 1:23), he promptly introduced them to Jesus. Isaiah also warned that to some people
the Lord would be 'a stone that causes men to stumble and a

rock that makes them fall' (Isaiah 8:14); and the apostle Peter applies these words directly to Jesus (see 1 Peter 2:8). One of the psalmists said of the Lord, 'In the beginning you laid the foundations of the earth, and the heavens are the work of your hands' (Psalm 102:25); and a New Testament writer uses those exact words about Jesus (see Hebrews 1:10). Writing of God's power and mercy, the prophet Joel said, 'Everyone who calls on the name of the LORD will be saved' (Joel 2:32); and both Peter (Acts 2:21) and Paul (Romans 10:13) quote Joel verbatim when writing about Jesus.

These examples are just the tip of the iceberg. Paul refers to Jesus as 'Lord' about 200 times. One of the most important of these is where he says that 'If you confess with your mouth, "Jesus is Lord," and believe in your heart that God raised him from the dead, you will be saved' (Romans 10:9). In what may be the first written Christian creed, this tells us that to confess 'Jesus is Lord' is to acknowledge that he 'shares the name and the nature, the holiness, the authority, power, majesty and eternity of the one and only true God'.[8] This is why Paul says elsewhere, 'Therefore I tell you that no one who is speaking by the Spirit of God says, "Jesus be cursed," and no one can say, "Jesus is Lord," except by the Holy Spirit' (1 Corinthians 12:3). Anybody can say the words, 'Jesus is Lord,' but nobody can submit himself to what that implies unless God the Holy Spirit is at work in his heart.

The living likeness

In the Bible, a person's name is often a reflection of his character or attributes. If Jesus possesses divine names and titles — and especially the sacred name 'Lord' — does he also possess God's attributes? The Bible's answer is an emphatic 'Yes!' Here are seven major attributes of God, matched by statements about Jesus.

God is eternal

The Bible calls him 'the eternal God' (Deuteronomy 33:27) and says that he is 'from everlasting to everlasting' (Psalm 90:2), beyond and above time, and having neither beginning nor end. God says, 'I am the Alpha and the Omega, who is, and who was, and who is to come, the Almighty' (Revelation 1:8); but in the same book Jesus says, 'I am the Alpha and the Omega, the First and the Last, the Beginning and the End' (Revelation 22:13). The point could hardly be clearer.

God is independent

Paul says that God 'is not served by human hands, as if he needed anything, because he himself gives all men life and breath and everything else' (Acts 17:25); and Jesus says of himself that he 'gives life to the world' (John 6:33).

God is holy

Isaiah tells of a vision in which he saw angels in heaven worshipping God and crying, 'Holy, holy, holy, is the LORD Almighty' (Isaiah 6:3), while elsewhere the Bible says that God is 'majestic in holiness' (Exodus 15:11); and Jesus is called 'the Holy One of God' (John 6:69). Incidentally, the word translated 'holy' means 'distinct' or 'different', and is an additional pointer to Jesus' identity.

God is everywhere

Rejoicing in the assurance that God is always present to guide and strengthen him, the psalmist asks God, 'Where can I go from your Spirit? Where can I flee from your presence?' (Psalm 139:7). Jesus promised the same constant help to his followers: 'I am with you always, to the very end of the age' (Matthew

28:20). Only someone who could be in every place at the same time could fulfil this promise.

God knows everything

He has perfect and eternal wisdom and knowledge. There is nothing that God can learn or discover. An Old Testament believer tells God, 'You alone know the hearts of all men' (1 Kings 8:39), and a New Testament writer says, 'Nothing in all creation is hidden from God's sight. Everything is uncovered and laid bare before the eyes of him to whom we must give account' (Hebrews 4:13). Yet the Bible attributes exactly the same qualities to Jesus. He 'knew all men' (John 2:24); he 'knew what was in a man' (John 2:25); and Paul speaks of him as the one 'in whom are hidden all the treasures of wisdom and knowledge' (Colossians 2:3).

God is all-powerful

He is the 'Lord God Almighty' (Revelation 19:6) who says, 'I am the LORD, the God of all mankind. Is anything too hard for me?' (Jeremiah 32:27). Yet during his earthly life Jesus demonstrated his power over disease, the devil, death and the natural elements, and claimed that 'All authority in heaven and on earth has been given to me' (Matthew 28:18).

God is unchangeable

He never varies, in essence, direction or purpose and 'does not change like shifting shadows' (James 1:17). In his own words, 'I the LORD do not change' (Malachi 3:6). But the Bible also says that although Jesus went through all the normal stages of human growth while here on earth, he remains 'the same yesterday and today and for ever' (Hebrews 13:8).

In becoming a man, Jesus apparently limited his use of some of these qualities. He became dependent on food, drink and sleep. He could not be in two places at once and asked questions, such as, 'Who touched my clothes?' (Mark 5:30) and 'How many loaves do you have?' (Mark 6:38). But his humanity never diluted his divinity. In his divine nature he remained eternal, independent, holy, omnipresent, all-knowing, all-powerful and unchangeable. Has any other human being possessed even one of these qualities?

Statements on status

As Jesus is given the same names and titles as God and is said to possess God's attributes, we should expect him to be given divine status by having his name linked with God's in some formal way — and this is what we find.

One of the last instructions Jesus gave his followers was to 'go and make disciples of all nations, baptizing them in the name of the Father and of the Son and of the Holy Spirit' (Matthew 28:19). Incidentally, this is one of the Bible's clearest statements of the fact that God exists in three persons — the Father, the Son and the Holy Spirit (now often collectively called the Holy Trinity). Notice how this comes across here. Christians are to be baptized in the *name* (singular) of three persons. In linking his own name with those of the Father and the Holy Spirit Jesus was obviously claiming equality with them. As someone has said, 'The union of these three names in the form of baptism proves that the Son and the Holy Spirit are equal with the Father. Nothing would be more absurd or blasphemous than to unite the name of a creature — a man or an angel — with the name of the ever-living God in this solemn rite.'[9]

The three divine names are also linked in the last words Paul wrote to the church at Corinth: 'May the grace of the Lord

Jesus Christ, and the love of God, and the fellowship of the Holy Spirit be with you all' (2 Corinthians 13:14). Here the name of Jesus comes first. Theologians usually speak of the three divine persons in the same order — Father, Son and Holy Spirit — but in the Bible this is not the case. There are twelve places in the New Testament where the three names are grouped together, yet they are arranged in six different ways, with each of the three names occupying each of the three places twice. This tells us that there is nothing sacred about the order. We must not think of any person in the Godhead as being inferior, or in any way less than fully God. For example, we must never think of the Father as 'senior' and the Son as in some way 'junior'. In the words of the great Athanasian Creed, which dates from about the fifth century, 'In this Trinity no one is first or last, no one is greater or less.' What is absolutely clear is that in Paul's words Jesus the eternal Son is given absolute equality within the Godhead.

Actions speak...

The Bible gives Jesus divine names, titles, attributes and status, but as actions are said to speak louder than words, is there any concrete evidence to back up these claims? We have already seen the significance of his healing miracles; now we can go far beyond these, because the Bible speaks of Jesus doing things that only God could do.

Creation

The Bible's opening words are, 'In the beginning God created the heavens and the earth' (Genesis 1:1); but Paul says of Jesus that 'By him all things were created: things in heaven and on earth, visible and invisible, whether thrones or powers or rulers

or authorities; all things were created by him and for him'
(Colossians 1:16). It would be impossible to be clearer or more
comprehensive than that! The same Jesus who was born as a
helpless baby at Bethlehem was the sovereign Creator of the
entire universe.

Preservation

When creation was complete, God did not act like an absentee
landlord and leave it to function on its own. Instead, he exer-
cises his almighty power both in upholding it and in ruling it in
sovereign authority: 'The LORD has established his throne in
heaven, and his kingdom rules over all' (Psalm 103:19). Yet the
Bible also says that it is Jesus who is 'sustaining all things by his
powerful word' (Hebrews 1:3), so that 'in him all things hold
together' (Colossians 1:17). It is Jesus who prevents our cos-
mos from becoming chaos. Every atom in the universe is held
together by his 'powerful word'. Who but God could possibly
do this?

Salvation

Not surprisingly, the Bible shows salvation to be an even greater
work than creation. Salvation rescues man from his greatest
enemy (the devil), overcomes the greatest resistance (his rebellious, sinful nature), solves his greatest problem (being separated
from God), prevents the greatest disaster (being eternally condemned) and brings the greatest blessings (the forgiveness of
sins and an eternal relationship with God). As we should expect, the Bible teaches that only God can bring anyone to salvation. David says that 'The salvation of the righteous comes
from the LORD' (Psalm 37:39) and God tells his people, 'You
shall acknowledge no God but me, no Saviour except me'
(Hosea 13:4).

In the Old Testament 'God' and 'Saviour' are virtually identical terms,[10] yet in the New Testament Jesus is seen to be that
Saviour. He said that he came into the world 'to seek and to
save what was lost' (Luke 19:10) and Paul made it clear that
'Christ Jesus came into the world to save sinners' (1 Timothy
1:15). John wrote, 'The Father has sent his Son to be the Saviour of the world' (1 John 4:14), and it was when writing of
Jesus that Peter confirmed, 'Salvation is found in no one else,
for there is no other name under heaven given to men by which
we must be saved' (Acts 4:12). In other words, 'Christ is the
final word about salvation. Here, he is not only without a peer,
he is without a competitor.'[11]

Forgiveness

Guilt is one of man's greatest problems and forgiveness one of
his greatest needs. Swiss psychiatrist Dr Paul Tournier wrote,
'We all know that guilt is no invention of the Bible or the church.
It is present universally in the human soul. And we cannot deal
with guilt without dealing with the religious questions it poses.'[12]
Tournier is right, but how can a God of perfect holiness, whose
righteous anger burns against all evil, forgive even one sin in
the life of even one person, let alone every sin in the lives of
millions? The Bible's unanimous answer to that question is that
Jesus dies in the place of sinners, taking upon himself God's
holy anger and judgement and becoming as accountable for
the sins of others as if he had been responsible for them, with
the result that God forgives every sinner for whom Jesus paid
sin's death penalty.

This is the background to an indirect claim to deity which
many people miss: *Jesus claimed to forgive people's sins.* You
might say, 'But forgiving sins is not a claim to deity. We are all
supposed to forgive people who sin against us. Surely that is all
that Jesus was doing?' That argument is easily squashed! When

four men brought their paralysed friend to Jesus in the hope that he might heal him, the first thing Jesus said to him was, 'Son, your sins are forgiven' (Mark 2:5). Jesus had never seen the man before, and his sins had not been committed against Jesus as a fellow human being. Yet Jesus told him that all his sins were forgiven — his guilt was gone; the slate was wiped clean. But unless Jesus was more than a man, how could he say that? How could he forgive sins that humanly speaking were none of his business? *A person can be forgiven only by the person he offends.* If your first words on being introduced to a stranger were 'I want you to know that all your sins are for-given,' the person concerned would make sure you remained a stranger! This is how C. S. Lewis puts it: 'We can all understand how a man forgives offences against himself. You tread on my toe and I forgive you, you steal my money and I forgive you. But what should we make of a man, himself unrobbed and untrodden on, who announced that he forgave you for tread-ing on other men's toes and stealing other men's money? Asin-ine fatuity is the kindest description we should give of such conduct. Yet this is what Jesus did. He told people that their sins were forgiven, and never waited to consult all the other people whom their sins had undoubtedly injured. He unhesi-tatingly behaved as if he was the party chiefly concerned, the person chiefly offended in all offences. This makes sense only if he really was the God whose laws are broken and whose love is wounded in every sin. In the mouth of any speaker who is not God, these words would imply what I can only regard as a silliness and conceit unrivalled by any other character in history.'[13]

The religious leaders listening to Jesus made a much more serious charge: 'Why does this fellow talk like that? He's blas-pheming! Who can forgive sins but God alone?' (Mark 2:6). They knew that all sin was against God, who alone could re-move the guilt and pardon the sinner. This was the basis for this moving invitation:

'Seek the LORD while he may be found;
    call on him, while he is near.
Let the wicked forsake his way
    and the evil man his thoughts.
Let him turn to the LORD, and *he* will have mercy on him,
    and to our God, for *he* will freely pardon'
                                            (Isaiah 55:6-7).

Jesus was claiming to do something that God alone had the right to do, and to the religious leaders this meant only one thing — blasphemy. Their theology was right, but their conclusion was wrong, and moments later Jesus healed the man's paralysis to demonstrate his authority. They could now see that Jesus had authority to deal with sickness; they should have sensed that he also had authority to deal with sin.

Eternal life

Salvation's ultimate blessing is eternal life, the essence of which is fellowship with God. This begins on earth when a person is saved and continues for ever in heaven, 'the home of righteousness' (2 Peter 3:13) where there will be 'no more death or mourning or crying or pain' (Revelation 21:4), and where God's people 'will reign for ever and ever' (Revelation 22:5). God alone has the authority and power to give eternal life; in the psalmist's words, 'The LORD bestows his blessing, even life for evermore' (Psalm 133:3). Yet Jesus claimed even this authority and power: 'The Son gives life to whom he is pleased to give it' (John 5:21). Elsewhere, he said of God's people, 'I give them eternal life, and they shall never perish; no one can snatch them out of my hand' (John 10:28). If Jesus is not God these words are ridiculous.

The same applies to other statements he made. He told his disciples that after his death God the Holy Spirit would come to guide, direct and strengthen them and to 'convict the world of guilt in regard to sin and righteousness and judgement' (John 16:8). That kind of statement could have been no more than a prediction by a prophet inspired by God, but in the same breath Jesus had just told them, *'I* will send him to you' (John 16:7). As the Holy Spirit is God, how can a mere man — even the greatest of men — 'send' him anywhere?

Jesus put all his actions in perspective when answering the charge of blasphemy for breaking the Sabbath: 'I tell you the truth, the Son can do nothing by himself; he can do only what he sees his Father doing; because whatever the Father does the Son also does' (John 5:19). By saying that he could do nothing by himself Jesus meant that he could do nothing independently of his Father *because their wills were in permanent unison.* The reason Jesus could do nothing by himself was not a lack of power, but a lack of desire! He did *only* what the Father did and *everything* the Father did. This can mean only one thing: 'Surely he who is so intimately connected with God that he does what God does, does all God does, does all in the same manner in which God does it; surely such a person cannot but be equal with God.'[14] Of all the biblical evidence for the deity of Jesus, nothing speaks louder than his actions.

Loose ends

We are nearly ready to face the biggest question of all in our search for 'the real Jesus', but notice how the statement that Jesus is God ties up all the loose ends from previous chapters.

In chapter 3 we saw that *Jesus was the Messiah and the Son of God.* But we also saw that the Messiah was to be a king whose throne would remain 'as long as the heavens endure' (Psalm 89:29), and that the Son, in a unique and intimate relationship, shared the Father's glory with him 'before the world began' (John 17:5). Applied to a mere man, those statements are absurd. They make sense only if Jesus is God.

In chapter 4 we saw that *Jesus was born of a virgin*, something unique in human culture. Yet the most amazing thing was the identity of the child: 'All this took place to fulfil what the Lord had said through the prophet: "The virgin will be with child and will give birth to a son, and they will call him Immanuel" — which means, "God with us"' (Matthew 1:22-23). God could arrange for thousands of babies to be born without human fathers, but this would not mean that any of them could be called 'God'. In the birth of Jesus we see an even greater miracle — God *himself becoming a man* (what theologians call the 'incarnation'). This is the only explanation of his being given the name 'Immanuel'. Jesus is not God's baby boy, he is the eternal God.

In chapter 5 we saw that *Jesus lived a perfect life* in complete obedience to God's will and without sin of any kind. That has important implications. How could he lie about his identity if he never lied about anything? *If he was not God, he was not good; if he was not good he was not God.* There is no room for manoeuvre here.

In chapter 6 we saw that *Jesus voluntarily died in the place of sinners*, bearing in his own body and spirit the divine punishment of their sins. This makes sense only when we accept that Jesus is God. He could bear the sins of others because as God the value of his sacrifice was *infinite*, and more than sufficient to redeem all those in whose place he died. Because Jesus was God there was no question of an innocent third party being immorally punished; *it was God himself who bore the penalty he laid down.* When Jesus died on the cross, 'God was reconciling the world to himself in Christ' (2 Corinthians 5:19). The Bible never says, 'God died,' because he 'alone is immortal' (1 Timothy 6:16). Nevertheless, the one who died in the place of others was God, who became a man in order to do so. He himself became the substitute for sinners and in dying in their place made 'a full, perfect and sufficient sacrifice, oblation and satisfaction for the sins of the whole world'.[15]

In chapter 7 we established that *Jesus rose bodily from the dead by his own power.* If he had been just a man this would have been impossible, but the Bible teaches that exactly the opposite is true, and that 'it was impossible for death to keep its hold on him' (Acts 2:24). But why 'impossible'? It was not because the body of Jesus possessed some supernatural power that death had not quite extinguished, but because *as God* Jesus had authority to lay his life down 'and authority to take it up again' (John 10:18). As Paul puts it, Jesus 'was declared with power to be the Son of God, by his resurrection from the dead' (Romans 1:4). The resurrection was the clinching confirmation of all his claims, including the one that he was more than a man.

The ultimate question

We have come a long way in our search for 'the real Jesus' and in this chapter alone have uncovered masses of crucial evidence, with his claims, his actions, his miracles, his acceptance of worship, his names, titles, status and attributes all pointing in the same direction. *But does the Bible say that Jesus is God?* Seven New Testament statements give us the answer.

- *'In the beginning was the Word, and the Word was with God, and the Word was God'* (John 1:1).

This tells us three things about Jesus ('the Word'). Firstly, his *eternality*: 'In the beginning' he already 'was'. Jesus existed before all creation, and was therefore uncreated and eternal. Secondly, his *personality*: he was 'with God'. One commentator translates the phrase as 'face to face with God'.[16] Although he had a separate personality of his own, the force of the word 'with' indicates that within the Godhead he existed in living, active, intimate fellowship. Thirdly, his *deity*: 'The Word was God.' Although Jesus was a separate person from the Father, he was not a separate being. The Word is not said to be 'a god' or 'the god', but *'God'*. He does not by himself make up the entire Godhead, but 'the divinity that belongs to the rest of the Godhead belongs also to him'.[17] Everything that could be said about the Father could be said about the Son. As B. B. Warfield puts it, 'In some sense distinguishable from God, he was in an equally true sense identifiable with God. There is but one eternal God; this eternal God, the Word is.'[18]

- *'No one has ever seen God, but God the only Son, who is at the Father's side, has made him known'* (John 1:18).

Nobody would have argued with John's first phrase because 'God is spirit' (John 4:24), and as such is 'invisible' (1 Timothy 1:17), neither had anybody ever 'seen' God in the sense of having an intimate knowledge of him. Yet John says that Jesus 'made him known'. The verb is one we would use about explaining the detailed meaning of a text. The Amplified Bible says that Jesus 'brought [God] out where he can be seen'. This is what Paul meant when he wrote that 'God, who said, "Let light shine out of darkness," made his light shine in our hearts to give us the light of the knowledge of the glory of God in the face of Christ' (2 Corinthians 4:6). We discover who and what God is by looking at Jesus.

- *'Be shepherds of the church of God, which he bought with his own blood'* (Acts 20:28).

This was part of Paul's farewell message to the church leaders at Ephesus. Its message and meaning are so powerful that critics have suggested that 'God' should read 'the Lord', but 'the church of the Lord' appears nowhere in the Bible, whereas 'the church of God' is one Paul used often. What is more, early church fathers used phrases such as 'the blood of God',[19] 'a crucified God'[20] and 'the precious and lordly blood of our God'[21] as if they had a biblical text in mind. Paul's use of 'God' in this particular sentence is so stunning that it is difficult to imagine anybody inserting it by mistake, and because God is pure spirit (and as such has no blood) the only possible explanation is that the person who shed his own, human blood on the cross is God the Son.

- *'Theirs are the patriarchs, and from them is traced the human ancestry of Christ, who is God over all, for ever praised! Amen'* (Romans 9:5).

This is the climax of a passage in which Paul has been expressing his anguished concern for the spiritual condition of his fellow Jews. Here, he highlights the reason for his agony: they are rejecting the Messiah whose human ancestry has its roots in their own nation. Yet this statement has also been under attack. Some critics have suggested that the last phrase should read something like this: '...the human ancestry of Christ. God over all be for ever praised! Amen.' Christ's deity is obliterated with a dot! — but this makes nonsense of the fact that Paul is writing with a broken heart. He speaks of having 'great sorrow and unceasing anguish' (Romans 9:1) and even says that if it were possible he would be willing to be 'cursed and cut off from Christ for the sake of my brothers, those of my own race' (Romans 9:3). He then agonizes over the tragic irony that the Jews are ignoring the unique privileges of their heritage, including the human ancestry of Christ: then suddenly (according to the critics) he does an emotional somersault and bursts out,

'God over all be for ever praised'! It makes much more sense if
we leave the punctuation as it is and accept Paul's words as a
clear, concise statement of the fact that Jesus is God.

- *'And again, when God brings his firstborn into the world, he*
  says,
    "Let all God's angels worship him."
  In speaking of the angels he says,
    "He makes his angels winds,
        his servants flames of fire."
  But about the Son he says,
    "Your throne, O God, will last for ever and ever,
    and righteousness will be the sceptre of your kingdom"'
                                                        (Hebrews 1:6-8).

The main theme of the letter to the Hebrews is the pre-eminence
of Jesus, the Son of God. In a passage shortly before the one I
have quoted the writer says that Jesus is 'as much superior to
the angels as the name he has inherited is superior to theirs'
(Hebrews 1:4). Now read our statement again, then ask yourself
these questions: Who is speaking? Of whom is he speaking?
What does he say about him? The answers to those questions
are so obvious, and the implication so clear, that one theologian commented, 'Those who deny our Lord's divinity have
been greatly perplexed by this passage.'[22] That is putting it
mildly!

- *'Your attitude should be the same as that of Christ Jesus:*
  Who, being in very nature God,
        did not consider equality with God something to be
        grasped,
  but made himself nothing,
        taking the very nature of a servant,

being made in human likeness.
And being found in appearance as a man,
  he humbled himself
  and became obedient to death — even death on a cross!
Therefore God exalted him to the highest place
  and gave him the name that is above every name,
that at the name of Jesus every knee should bow,
  in heaven and on earth and under the earth,
and every tongue confess that Jesus Christ is Lord,
  to the glory of God the Father'

(Philippians 2:5-11).

This is one of the fullest New Testament statements on our subject and demands closer examination. The context is Paul's concern that the Christians at Philippi should be humble, unselfish and concerned for the well-being of others, and in handling this pastoral issue he uses Jesus as an illustration of what he wants to say. This makes his statement even more impressive, because although one of the greatest in Scripture, it is indirect, almost incidental. For our present purposes we need concentrate only on the first part, in which Paul says six things about Jesus.

Firstly, he introduces him as 'being in very nature God', telling us that Jesus is everything that God is. 'He is declared, in the most express manner possible, to be all that God is, to possess the whole fulness of attributes which make God God.'[23] There could hardly be a more concise statement that Jesus is eternally, truly, totally God.

Secondly, Jesus 'did not consider equality with God something to be grasped'. The word 'equality' comes from the Greek *isos* from which we get words like 'isosceles' (an isosceles triangle is one with two equal sides) and 'isobar' (a line on a map connecting points of barometric pressure). It was the root of the word used by those who accused Jesus of blasphemy by 'making himself *equal* with God' (John 5:18).

Nothing in Jesus' nature fell short of the nature of God, yet Jesus did not consider this equality with God 'something to be grasped'. He did not hang on to it as if it were the only thing that mattered. Instead, he considered that he had a greater priority than his own uninterrupted glory, and in the interests of others he deliberately and voluntarily set it aside.

Thirdly, 'he made himself nothing'. This is a very poor rendering of words that literally mean 'he emptied himself'. This does not mean that he gave up any of the qualities or attributes that made him God, as the Bible makes it clear that he retained his deity throughout his earthly life. Then in what ways did he 'empty himself'? He obviously laid aside the majesty and glory that were his in heaven — the glory he had with his Father 'before the world began' (John 17:5) — though it seems that it almost broke through like a sudden burst of sunshine on a cloudy day, when he was transfigured, and 'his face shone like the sun, and his clothes became as white as the light' (Matthew 17:2). He also gave up his privileges, 'the shared riches of the heavenly places',[24] and accepted the limitations of life on earth. In Paul's words, 'For you know the grace of our Lord Jesus Christ, that though he was rich, yet for your sakes he became poor, so that you through his poverty might become rich' (2 Corinthians 8:9). He chose to be born as a baby, live as a man, suffer as an outcast and die like a criminal. He exchanged the homage of angels for the hatred of men, a crown for a cross, glory for the grave.

Fourthly, he made himself nothing by 'taking the very nature of a servant'. Just as he was in very nature God, so he took the 'very nature' of a servant. He was not play-acting. He became as fully an earthly servant as he had been a heavenly sovereign. He became the servant of his heavenly Father, completely submissive to his will; this explains why he said that 'The Father is greater than I' (John 14:28). As his Father's servant, Jesus gave up the independent exercise of his own authority and power; this explains why he said, 'The Son can do nothing by himself' (John 5:19). But he also became the servant of mankind. In his own words, 'The Son of Man did not come to be served, but to serve, and to give his life as a ransom for many' (Mark 10:45). The Bible gives us a superb illustration of this in describing a final meal with his disciples: 'Jesus knew that the Father had put all things under his power, and that he had come from God and was returning to God; so he got up from the meal, took off his outer clothing, and wrapped a towel round his waist. After that, he poured water into a basin and began to wash his disciples' feet, drying them with the towel that was wrapped around him' (John 13:3-5). When Peter protested that Jesus should not wash his feet, Jesus replied, 'You do not realize now what I am doing, but later you will understand' (John 13:7). On the brink of his greatest act as a servant (the laying down of his life) Jesus gave his disciples this dramatic 'visual aid' of his true servanthood. He washed their feet — yet it had been his divine power that had created every drop of water in the universe and his wisdom that had determined its content and characteristics.

Fifthly, Jesus was 'made in human likeness'. This does not mean that Jesus was created or in some way 'manufactured'. The literal meaning of 'made' is that he 'came to be'. Jesus became something he had never been before. In becoming a man, Jesus did not become something *less*, but something *more*. He remained God, with all the glory that belongs to God, and became man, with all the glory that belongs to man. He remained everything involved in being divine and at the same time became everything involved in being human. J. I. Packer sums it up like this: 'Here are two mysteries for the price of one

— the plurality of persons within the unity of God, and the union of Godhead and manhood in the person of Jesus ... God became man; the divine Son became a Jew; the Almighty appeared on earth as a helpless human baby, unable to do more than lie and stare and wriggle and make noises, needing to be fed and changed and taught to talk like any other child. And there was no illusion or deception in this: the babyhood of the Son of God was a reality. The more you think about it, the more staggering it gets. Nothing in fiction is so fantastic as is this truth of the incarnation.'[25]

Sixthly, he was 'found in appearance as a man'. Paul is not saying that Jesus was *not* a man, but that outwardly he seemed to be nothing more. He did not have a halo, or wings, or a supernatural glow to his skin. He ate, drank, walked, worked and slept just like anyone else. Yet he was not merely what he appeared to be; *there was more to him than met the eye.* He was similar to other men, yet not the same, because he was not merely a man.

In the remainder of the passage we are told that having become a man Jesus humbled himself and became obedient even to the extent of dying on a cross, as a result of which he was raised from the dead and ascended into heaven, where he is rightly worshipped as Lord. This is the climax of a powerful passage throughout which one message comes through loud and clear: *Jesus is God.*

- '*For in Christ all the fulness of the Deity lives in bodily form*' (Colossians 2:9)

In some ways, this is an even more impressive statement than the previous one, because it crams so much into so little. G. Campbell Morgan wrote that in this sentence the truth about Jesus 'is focused, crystallized, stated with a brevity and a conciseness that is full and final'.[26] It could certainly not be clearer. Not only did Jesus possess God's wisdom, power, knowledge and all other attributes; he possessed deity — *fulness* of deity — *all* the fulness of deity. When Jesus became a man there was no *subtraction*. He remained God in all his fulness. There was a time when Jesus was God but not man, but never a time when Jesus was man but not God. Nor was there *division*. Jesus did not give up any of his Godhood to make room for his manhood. As we look at him, he does not fall to pieces in our hands, some parts human and others divine. Neither did he become a mixture of God and man; his deity was not humanized, nor was his humanity deified. He remained fully divine throughout his earthly life, and his agreement to die underlined this. Other men have no choice in the matter.

What happened when Jesus became a man was not subtraction or division but *addition*. He took upon himself human nature, which he had never previously possessed. He added humanity to his deity, and from then on has remained both God and man, with two natures in one personality. The one who died on the cross, rose again and ascended into heaven is still a man, in whom it is still true to say that 'all the fulness of the deity lives in bodily form'. No wonder Campbell Morgan added, 'I do not hesitate to say that this statement is either the most stupendous statement about Christ in all the universe of God, or it is the most fatuous and deplorable lie that was ever written by the stylus of a human being.'[27]

We have looked at seven major New Testament statements that indicate that Jesus is God, but there are many other places in which the same truth is stated or implied. Paul says that Jesus is 'the image of the invisible God' (Colossians 1:15) and that 'God was pleased to have all his fulness dwell in him' (Colossians 1:19). He says that 'God appeared in a body' (1 Timothy 3:16) and he looks forward to 'the glorious appearing of our great God and Saviour, Jesus Christ' (Titus 2:13). Peter speaks of 'the righteousness of our God and Saviour Jesus Christ' (2 Peter 1:1). John calls Jesus 'the true God and eternal life' (1 John 5:20). The writer of Hebrews describes him as 'the radiance of God's glory and the exact representation of his being' (Hebrews 1:3). If these are not expressions of the same truth, it is difficult to know what they are!

Conclusion of the case

By any human reckoning the weight and consistency of the evidence that Jesus is God is overpowering. The issue is not merely 'beyond all reasonable doubt', but beyond doubt of any kind. What is more, the evidence exceeds all human criteria, because every sentence of it comes from the Bible, 'the living and enduring word of God' (1 Peter 1:23). It is as if God himself has been in the witness box, giving evidence on his own behalf, and the fact that 'it is impossible for God to lie' (Hebrews 6:18) means that every word of the evidence is rock solid. No amount of cross-examination can ever shake it, and all other witnesses are found to be false.

You have now read eight whole chapters of clear and consistent evidence. *Now you must decide what to do with it.* The options are simple and the implications stupendous. The final chapter spells them out.

9.

The verdict

One of the most dramatic moments in any court case is when the jury retires to consider its verdict. The witnesses have been heard, the questions posed, the arguments presented. Now comes the crunch: *what will be the verdict?* We have reached a similar point in this book, because there is a sense in which Jesus of Nazareth has been on trial. We have examined his background, birth, life, character and teaching, as well as the events surrounding his death, yet our purpose has not been to assess his impact or his ideals but to establish his identity: *who is the real Jesus?*

You, the jury

The issue was exactly the same when he went on trial nearly 2,000 years ago. After his arrest he was taken before a Jewish high priest Annas for a preliminary hearing, and then to another, Caiaphas, who got straight to the point: 'I charge you under oath by the living God: Tell us if you are the Christ, the Son of God' (Matthew 26:63). Next, he was dragged before Pontius Pilate, the Roman governor, where the Jewish charge of treason was based on the fact that 'he ... claims to be Christ, a king' (Luke 23:2). When Pilate eventually told the Jews, 'I

find no basis for a charge against him' (John 19:6) they insisted,
'We have a law, and according to that law he must die, because
he claimed to be the Son of God' (John 19:7). The law they
had in mind said, 'Anyone who blasphemes the name of the
LORD must be put to death' (Leviticus 24:16). As the charge
was blasphemy, the issue was clearly his identity. It still is — but
while the accused and the issue remain the same, you have
taken the place of Annas, Caiaphas and Pilate.

In reading this book you have listened to many witnesses
and heard masses of evidence, including over 500 direct statements from Scripture. Now you must consider your verdict. As
you do, let me remind you that the issue is not the circumstances of Jesus' birth, nor the quality of his teaching, nor the
significance of his miracles, nor the way he died, nor the extraordinary business of his resurrection. Each of these has a bearing on the case, but what you are being asked to consider is
this: who is he? More specifically, is he or is he not the divine
person he claimed to be? There can obviously be only one of
two possible answers: 'Yes' or 'No'. Either Jesus is God, or he is
not. What is your verdict?

Devil in disguise?

Some people may be prepared to bring in a 'No' verdict without giving the matter much thought, but that makes no sense,
and it leaves the problem of explaining away his claims. There
are just three ways of trying to do this.

The first is to say that Jesus was evil. In other words, he
knew perfectly well that he was not the Son of God, but deliberately tried to hoodwink his fellow Jews, who were longing for
the Old Testament prophecies to be fulfilled. Think of the extent
of evil involved here. Firstly, he would have been a serial liar.
When he said that his words were on a par with the teaching of

the Old Testament, he was lying. When he claimed the right to forgive sins, he was lying. When he claimed to share God's nature, he was lying. When he said he had authority to give eternal life, he was lying. When he said, 'I am ... the truth...' (John 14:6), he was lying. When he said he would die in the place of others, he was lying. But if he was lying on these issues it is difficult to see how we can trust a single word he said. Again, if he knew he was making false claims to deity, he would have been an outrageous *blasphemer*. In the Old Testament blasphemy was 'an act of effrontery in which the honour of God is insulted by man'[1] — and a capital offence under Jewish law. This explains why the Jews were constantly baying for his blood.

He would also have been a *hypocrite*, preaching one thing but practising another; teaching humility, yet arrogantly accepting other men's worship; teaching honesty, yet lying about his own identity.

In addition, he would have been a *deceiver*. His teaching about forgiveness and eternal life touched the deepest areas of human need. He spoke to people who were conscious of their sin, fearful of judgement and longing to know how they could find peace with God. What is more, they were 'harassed and helpless, like sheep without a shepherd' (Matthew 9:36), groaning under the burden of religious rules and regulations which brought them no relief. To people like this Jesus said, 'Friend, your sins are forgiven' (Luke 5:20); 'Your faith has saved you; go in peace' (Luke 7:50); 'The words I have spoken to you are spirit and they are life' (John 6:63). But if Jesus was not God, these words were meaningless, empty, wicked and cruel. Anybody guilty of such wholesale lying, blasphemy, hypocrisy, and cruel deceit and cruelty would have been demonically evil.

How does that tie in with what we see of his character on the pages of the New Testament? Here we find someone who is loving, gracious, compassionate, gentle, sympathetic, balanced

and controlled. Are these the marks of demon possession? And
if Jesus was so riddled with evil, how do we explain his amazing influence for good. Even people with no Christian axe to
grind have been forced to acknowledge this. The nineteenth-
century historian William Lecky, a persistent opponent of Christianity, admitted that Jesus was not only 'the highest pattern of
virtue, but the strongest incentive to its practice... The simple
record of these three short years of active life has done more to
regenerate and soften mankind than all the disquisitions [i.e.
essays] of philosophers and all the exhortations of moralists.'[2]
The Jewish thinker Claude Montefiore said that Jesus 'exer-
cised a greater influence on mankind and civilization than any
other person' and that 'his life and character have been regarded by almost all the best and wisest people who have heard
or read of his actions and his words as the greatest religious
exemplar [i.e. example] of every age'.[3]

There are millions of people alive today who quietly claim
that Jesus has transformed their moral and spiritual lives, and
there have been countless millions of others over the course of
the last 2,000 years who have made the same claim. In the
nineteenth century alone Lord Shaftesbury revolutionized Britain's approach to the mentally ill, the homeless, women and
children working in coal mines and children working in factor-
ies; Thomas Barnado set up his network of orphanages; Elizabeth Fry triggered off widespread prison reform; William
Wilberforce brought about the abolition of the slave trade in
Britain and Jean Henri Dunant wrote a book[4] that led to the
founding of the International Red Cross. These all claimed that
Jesus was the major influence in their private lives and the
motivating force behind their public service — but if Jesus was
rotten to the core these claims are bizarre. In his own words, 'A
good tree cannot bear bad fruit, and a bad tree cannot bear
good fruit' (Matthew 7:18).

Right but wrong?

The second theory to consider if Jesus was not God is that
although he was a good man and a fine moral teacher *he was
deluded about his own identity*. Dismissing his claims without
denouncing his character sounds a more promising line, but it
is easier said than done for one major reason — his teaching
and his claims were welded together. For example, he repeatedly endorsed Old Testament teaching, but also said, 'These
are the Scriptures that testify about *me*' (John 5:39). Again, he
frequently spoke about the kingdom of God (or the kingdom of
heaven) and then went on to link himself to everything the
kingdom meant. The Old Testament taught that sickness, sin
and death would be abolished when the kingdom of God was
fully revealed, and Jesus began his ministry by crying, 'Repent,
for the kingdom of heaven is near' (Matthew 4:17). He easily
demolished his opponents' ridiculous suggestion that he was
using demonic power to cast out demons, and then added,
'But if I drive out demons by the Spirit of God, then the kingdom of God has come upon you' (Matthew 12:28).

He spoke not only of 'the kingdom of God', but of *his* kingdom, and inferred that they were identical. When Pilate asked
him if he was the king of the Jews he replied that his kingdom
was eternal — 'My kingdom is not of this world' (John 18:36).
This ties in exactly with Old Testament prophecies that the
Messiah would rule over 'an everlasting dominion that will not
pass away', a kingdom 'that will never be destroyed' (Daniel
7:14). It also fits in with the angel's promise before his birth that
'His kingdom will never end' (Luke 1:33).

Jesus wove these themes so closely into his teaching that it
is impossible to separate them. As historian Kenneth Scott
Latourette says, 'It must be obvious to any thoughtful reader of
the Gospels that Jesus regarded himself and his message as

inseparable. He was a great teacher, but he was more. His teaching about the kingdom of God, about human conduct and about God were important but they could not be divorced from him without, from his standpoint, being vitiated [i.e. weakened].'[5] *If you take away the things Jesus said about himself, directly or indirectly, his teaching loses virtually all of its impact.* C. S. Lewis puts it like this: 'I am trying here to prevent anyone saying the really foolish thing that people often say about him: "I'm ready to accept Jesus as a great moral teacher, but I don't accept his claim to be God." A man who was merely a man and said the sort of things Jesus said would not be a great moral teacher... Let us not come up with any patronizing nonsense about his being a great human teacher. He has not left that open to us. He did not intend to.'[6] Jesus was either much more than a great teacher or he was much less. To say that he was right in most of his teaching but wrong in its greatest theme is neither sensible nor honest.

Another poached egg?

The third alternative is straightforward enough: *he was mentally deranged.* Insanity is both frightening and mysterious, and sometimes leads people to make the most absurd claims about themselves. Sir Norman Anderson tells of playing football for his school against a team from what was then known as a lunatic asylum. One of the patients there firmly believed that he was a poached egg.[7] Religious mania has often led to claims that are equally ridiculous, but these claims are matched by character traits in the people concerned. Imbalance in the mind affects a person's feet and hands, not just his mouth, and we can test the theory that Jesus was insane by seeing whether he fits the pattern.

What about his life? Is this a lunatic we see healing the sick, feeding the hungry, encouraging the sad and comforting the bereaved? Far from being fragmented, irrational, eccentric and taken up with his own needs, we find him balanced, composed and constantly concerned with the well-being of others. What about his teaching? Is the Lord's Prayer the product of a disturbed mind? Is the Sermon on the Mount an expression of insanity? If so, we urgently need a global epidemic of it! When Jesus spoke of laying down his own life and taking it up again, some people said, 'He is demon-possessed and raving mad. Why listen to him?' (John 10:20). The answer to their question came three days after they had killed him. The person who examines the character of Jesus, listens to his words, watches his actions and concludes that the man is a maniac is telling us nothing about Jesus, but a great deal about himself!

Why bother?

We have now eliminated the only three theories that would allow the conclusion that Jesus was not the divine person he claimed to be. This leaves only one alternative: *Jesus is God.*

Having heard the witnesses, listened to the arguments and sifted the evidence, *what do you say?* At this point you might be asking, 'Does it matter? Why should I have to make up my mind one way or the other?' There is a sense in which that may be true about some of the facts contained in the Bible; the dimensions of Noah's ark, details of John the Baptist's diet, and the casualty figures in Old Testament battles can never significantly affect you. But the identity of Jesus is in a different category altogether, because as he himself put it, *'If you do not believe that I am the one I claim to be, you will ... die in your sins'* (John 8:24). The last two words, 'your sins', ought to be enough to get any honest person's attention, because 'there is no one who does not sin' (1 Kings 8:46). When Solomon asks, 'Who can say, "I have kept my heart pure; I am clean and without sin"?' (Proverbs 20:9), the only honest response is guilty silence. Do you agree? Or do you claim to be perfect in everything you think, say and do? The Bible says, 'Whoever keeps the whole law and yet stumbles at just one point is guilty of breaking all of it' (James 2:10). God's law forbids both adultery and murder, and the adulterer will not escape God's judgement on the basis that he has never committed murder, nor will anyone get away with murder as long as he has never committed adultery. God's law is not like a pile of stones, from which you can remove one or two without doing any harm; it is like a pane of glass — one crack and the whole pane is broken.

There is no such thing as a 'minor offence' against the majesty of God. This comes across in the Bible when what some might consider 'small' sins are linked with others. Here are two examples. Paul wrote that the lives of some of his contemporaries 'have become filled with every kind of wickedness, evil, greed and depravity. They are full of envy, murder, strife, deceit and malice. They are *gossips*, slanderers, God-haters, insolent, arrogant and boastful; they invent ways of doing evil; they disobey their parents; they are senseless, faithless, heartless, ruthless' (Romans 1:29-31). At about the same time he told the Christians at Corinth, 'Do you not know that the wicked will not inherit the kingdom of God? Do not be deceived: Neither the sexually immoral nor idolaters nor adulterers nor male prostitutes nor homosexual offenders nor thieves nor the *greedy* nor drunkards nor slanderers nor swindlers will inherit the kingdom of God' (1 Corinthians 6:9-10). Notice the words I have emphasized. We would not put gossips in the same league as God-haters, or lump greed and idolatry together; but God does! All sins, even those we may think of as trivial, are capital offences against God and his glory.

This means that no one can get right with God by turning over a new leaf and cancelling out his vices by his virtues. The person who tries to do so is 'required to obey *the whole law*' (Galatians 5:3), and the Bible adds, 'All who rely on observing the law are under a curse, for it is written: "Cursed is everyone who does not continue to do *everything* written in the Book of the Law"' (Galatians 3:10). To satisfy God by your own efforts you would have to be perfect. Respectability is a useless substitute.

Now where do you stand? Have you avoided gross sins such as murder and adultery? Even when we read that Jesus taught that hatred is as sinful as murder and impure thinking the mental equivalent of adultery! And what about other sins such as pride, envy, greed, selfishness, bitterness, anger, covetousness and jealousy? What about sins of the tongue, such as lying, slander, gossip, destructive criticism, unkindness and swearing? And what about those things you have *failed* to do? The Bible says, 'Anyone, then, who knows the good he ought to do and doesn't do it, sins' (James 4:17). Have you always done all the good things you possibly could?

You may say, 'My moral guidelines are the Ten Commandments.' Then do you keep them? Is God always first in your life? Do you never misuse his name? Do you remember the Sabbath day 'by keeping it holy' (Exodus 20:8)? Have you never been dishonest or covetous? Jesus summarized the Ten Commandments in two sentences: 'Love the Lord your God with all your heart and with all your soul and with all your mind and with all your strength,' and 'Love your neighbour as yourself' (Mark 12:30-31). Are you seriously claiming that you have always done these things?

You may say, 'But my religion is the Sermon on the Mount.' Then do you live up to it? Do you 'hunger and thirst for righteousness' (Matthew 5:6)? Are you 'pure in heart' (Matthew 5:8)? How do you match up to the command: 'Be perfect, therefore, as your heavenly Father is perfect' (Matthew 5:48)? And what about the so-called 'Golden Rule': 'In everything, do to others what you would have them do to you' (Matthew 7:12)? Have you always obeyed that — in *everything*? There is only one honest response to questions like these: 'I have sinned against the LORD' (2 Samuel 12:13).

When we pull all of this together the picture becomes horrific. Imagine that you have sinned — by thought, word or deed, by what you have done or not done — just once a day. That comes to seven times in a week, 365 times in a year and 25,550 in a lifetime of seventy years. But can you honestly say that your life has had only one imperfection a day? Is one an hour not closer to the truth? That means twenty-four in a day, 168 in a week, 8,736 in a year and 611,520 in seventy years. Yet even that is not the whole picture, because 'all have sinned and *fall* short of the glory of God' (Romans 3:23). Even at our best we come short of what God deserves, desires and demands. One Old Testament writer wrote, 'All of us have become like one who is unclean, and all our righteous acts are like filthy rags' (Isaiah 64:6). Surely you must agree with this? Have you *nothing* of which you should be ashamed? Would you be happy to have *every* detail of your life shared with everybody you know?

We saw earlier that sin inevitably cuts a person off from God, not only in this life but in the life to come. It is impossible to escape the Bible's emphasis on this. Jesus spoke more about hell than about heaven, constantly warning men of its reality and terror. He said it was a 'place of torment' (Luke 16:28) and a 'fiery furnace' (Matthew 13:42), where there would be 'weeping and gnashing of teeth' (Matthew 22:13) and where 'the fire never goes out' (Mark 9:43). This is something of what Jesus meant when he said that 'You will die in your sins.' Even one sin would be sufficient to keep you out of heaven — '*Nothing* impure will *ever* enter it' (Revelation 21:27) — but to 'die in your sins' means to die with all the accumulation of your sins standing between you and God and condemning you to be 'punished with everlasting destruction ... from the presence of the Lord and from the majesty of his power' (2 Thessalonians 1:9). Hell has been called 'the ultimate horror of God's universe'.⁸ It is also the inescapable and eternal punishment which God righteously inflicts on all who die in their sins.

Sin above all sins

Yet there is one sin above all others which Jesus says will condemn you. He says that you will die in your sins, 'if you do not believe that I am the one I claim to be' (John 8:24). However religious a person may be, however concerned to please God, however determined to live a good life, however diligent in his responsibilities within his family circle or in society at large, he will spend eternity in hell if he does not believe that Jesus is God. This may sound like horrifying overkill on God's part, but only if we fail to grasp what is involved in refusing to acknowledge that Jesus is divine.

Let me emphasize this in very direct and personal terms. If you reject the deity of Jesus, you are at odds with God the Father, because about the Son he says, 'Your throne, O God, will last for ever and ever' (Hebrews 1:8). Disagreeing with God the Father about the identity of his one and only Son is hardly trivial! You are also in direct conflict with Jesus himself, who said, 'He who is not with me is against me' (Luke 11:23). It is impossible to be neutral on the issue, and equally impossible to be 'with' Jesus while rejecting everything he said about himself. It also means that you are opposed to God the Holy Spirit, because in writing the Bible 'Men spoke from God as they were carried along by the Holy Spirit' (2 Peter 1:21). Jesus said that the Holy Spirit is 'the Spirit of truth' who would 'testify about me' (John 15:26) and rejecting that testimony has appalling consequences: 'Anyone who speaks against the Holy Spirit will not be forgiven, *either in this age or in the age to come*' (Matthew 12:32). These are some of the most solemn words in Scripture. If you come to the conclusion that Jesus was demonic, deluded or demented, when the Holy Spirit says he is divine, *not even God will ever be able to forgive you.*

The last paragraph points to that fact that men and women are condemned not only because of an accumulation of *sins*, but especially for the one great *sin* of refusing to accept the truth about Jesus. Jesus spoke not only of people dying in their *sins*; he also told those who were rejecting him, 'You will die in your *sin*' (John 8:21), showing that this was the greatest sin of all, sufficient to condemn them even if they lived otherwise perfect lives. He said the same kind of thing when teaching that the work of the Holy Spirit was to 'convict the world of guilt in regard to sin ... because men do not believe in me' (John 16:8-9). The Holy Spirit points out every sin, but the sin which lies behind all others is the refusal to acknowledge that Jesus Christ is Lord.

If this is still true of you, then Jesus made it clear that you are under God's judgement even as you read these words: 'Whoever believes in [God's Son] is not condemned, but whoever does not believe *stands condemned already* because he has not believed in the name of God's one and only Son' (John 3:18). What is more, that condemnation will be confirmed for ever when you come face to face with God on the Day of Judgement. Jesus said, 'There is a judge for the one who rejects me and does not accept my words; that very word which I spoke will condemn him at the last day. For I did not speak of my own accord, but the Father who sent me commanded me what to say and how to say it' (John 12:48-49). Nothing could be more terrifying or hopeless than to face a holy God on that terrible day knowing that here on earth you had deliberately rejected

everything he had said about his Son! Unlike a jury in a normal
trial, *you* are the one affected by your verdict — and the effects
will last for ever.

 · If you are still not convinced that Jesus is God, turn back to
the beginning of this chapter and read it again, slowly, carefully
and honestly. The issue is so important and the implications
are so far-reaching that you dare not come to the wrong conclusion. In spiritual terms it is a matter of life or death; it deter-
mines whether you are on your way to heaven or hell. How
can you possibly leave that issue in the balance?

Believing and believing

But perhaps you need not go back to the beginning of the chapter because as you have read through this book you have come
to see that Jesus is exactly who the Bible says he is, the living
and eternal God. You may have started reading as someone
who thought Jesus was no more than an exceptionally good
man, or a fine moral and spiritual teacher; now you have become convinced of his deity. If so, you have taken a great step
forward, *but it is not enough to save you from hell or take you
to heaven.* This is because when the Bible speaks of 'believing'
in Jesus Christ it means much more than accepting that what it
says about him is true. Jesus is not a logical proposition, but a
living person, and he demands a response that goes far beyond giving your approval to a list of facts about him. Jesus will
not be fobbed off by either your compliments or your convictions. There is a vital difference between 'believing' and 'believing', and the Bible illustrates it in several ways.

   A religious teacher once agreed with Jesus that 'God is one
and there is no other but him', yet at the end of their talk Jesus
told him, 'You are not far from the kingdom of God' (Mark
12:32-34). That was both an encouragement and a warning.

Jesus was encouraging the man to build on the foundation of the truth he had discovered; but he was also warning him that even his excellent grasp of the truth still left him outside God's kingdom. This man rejected atheism (which says there is no God), scepticism (which says there might be) and polytheism (which says there are many gods). He was convinced there was only one God, yet this conviction was not sufficient to save him.

Elsewhere, the Bible puts it even more strikingly: 'You believe that there is one God. Good! Even the demons believe that — and shudder' (James 2:19). Here again, the word 'believe' means accepting truth — in this case the fundamental Old Testament doctrine that 'The LORD our God, the LORD is one' (Deuteronomy 6:4). That belief is commended, but is immediately followed by the devastating comment, 'Even the demons believe that — and shudder.' This is illustrated in the Gospels. When two demon-possessed men met Jesus at Gadara they shouted, 'What do you want with us, Son of God?' (Matthew 8:29). On another occasion evil spirits fell down before him and cried out, 'You are the Son of God' (Mark 3:11). But the Gospels go even further and tell us that when confronting Jesus in the desert, Satan himself introduced two of his temptations with the words, 'If you are the Son of God...' (Matthew 4:3,6). The meaning of 'If...' is obviously 'Since...'; it was because Satan *knew* that Jesus was the Son of God that he tempted him in the way that he did.

This tells us that *there are no atheists in hell*. Even the devil and the evil spirits 'believe' in the sense of knowing that there is only one God. They know that Jesus is God's eternal Son, and that he was born of the virgin Mary, lived a perfect life, died in the place of sinners, rose again from the dead and ascended triumphantly into heaven, *but none of this knowledge does them any good*. Instead, the demons 'shudder in terror' when confronted with the reality of God's existence, knowing that their rebellion against him has left them condemned for ever. Just as a person can believe in God's existence yet ignore his claims, so a person can believe everything the Bible says about Jesus and still refuse to obey his teaching. But to do so is to be guilty of the fundamental sin we examined earlier, because 'The root of sin lies in the desire of men to live their lives in self-centred independence, disowning any allegiance to Jesus.'[9]

Those last three words point us towards what the Bible means by the kind of 'believing' God demands. When the Bible speaks about 'believing' in the Lord Jesus Christ it uses the word in a way in which it had never before been used. Literally, the word means 'trusting', something that involves not merely the mind but the will. It speaks of committing oneself to Jesus, clinging to him, relying on him. It is not just a question of assent, but of trust and obedience. Paul speaks of the eternal punishment of those 'who do not know God and do not *obey* the gospel of our Lord Jesus' (2 Thessalonians 1:8). In a normal court case the jury's responsibility ends the moment the verdict is given, but that is not so here. Even if your verdict is the right one, and you acknowledge that Jesus is God, you still have a responsibility to 'obey the gospel' by your wholehearted commitment to him as Saviour and Lord.

Moment of truth

In writing this book I have been praying that many who read it will come to this moment of truth. If you have, let me urge you to obey the gospel by turning to the Lord Jesus Christ, even as you read these closing pages. When Paul left Ephesus he reminded his friends there that he had just one message for all his hearers: they 'must turn to God in repentance and have faith in our Lord Jesus' (Acts 20:21). My message to you is exactly the same, because this is what God requires of you. The Bible says that 'This is [God's] *command*: to believe in the name of his Son, Jesus Christ' (1 John 3:23); and that 'God ... now ... *commands* all people everywhere to repent' (Acts 17:30). These are not options, they are orders, and to disobey them has fearful and eternal consequences. Let me take up these two commands, link them to the two titles 'Saviour' and 'Lord' that I used of Jesus in the previous paragraph, and urge you to obey them with all your heart.

1. *Turn to Jesus and trust him as your Saviour*

Some people think of turning to God only when they get into some kind of trouble, such as sickness or financial difficulties. But that insults God by treating him as no more than a heavenly health service or celestial cash dispenser. It is certainly true that God 'gives all men life and breath and everything else' (Acts 17:25), but he is under no obligation to heal your body, ease your pain, lengthen your life, save your marriage or boost your bank balance — nor is he at your beck and call to do any of these things. Your greatest need, and God's greatest concern, goes far beyond these. Your greatest need is to be saved from the guilt, power and consequences of your sin, and God promises to meet that need if you put your trust in the Lord Jesus Christ. Here are some of the ways in which this promise is worded in the Bible: 'For God so loved the world that he gave his one and only Son, that whoever believes in him shall not perish but have eternal life' (John 3:16). 'Whoever believes in the Son has eternal life' (John 3:36). 'Believe in the Lord Jesus, and you will be saved' (Acts 16:31). In other places the Bible speaks of the specific blessings that will be yours as you put your trust in Christ. You will be '*justified* by faith in Christ' (Galatians 2:16). You will receive '*redemption* through his blood, *the forgiveness of sins*, in accordance with the riches of God's grace' (Ephesians 1:7). You will have '*peace with God* through our Lord Jesus Christ' (Romans 5:1). You will join those who rejoice in the assurance that 'God has given us *eternal life*, and this life is in his Son' (1 John 5:11).

Yet these will be yours only if you turn wholeheartedly to Christ: 'Salvation is found in no one else, for there is no other name under heaven given to men by which we must be saved' (Acts 4:12). Turning to Jesus and trusting in him implies turning away from trusting in anything or anyone else. You must abandon whatever confidence you are placing in your own so-called goodness and recognize that all the good things you have done are utterly worthless as far as making you right with God is concerned. Just as Paul did, you must 'consider them rubbish' (Philippians 3:8).

This specifically includes abandoning all confidence in your religion. Make sure that you understand what this means. Gather up in your mind all the religious things you have ever done — every service you have attended, every prayer you have uttered, every word of Scripture you have ever read, every moment of time you have given to the church, every penny you have given to religious causes — then realize that in terms of making you right with God all of these are useless and can never make you acceptable in the sight of God. Even if you were to continue these with great regularity and sincerity to the end of your life, you would remain in the lost condition in which you were born. These things are not wrong in themselves. It is right to go to church, read the Bible, pray, and so on, but these activities cannot save you. If they could, God would not have sent his Son to die for man's salvation. The Bible says, 'There is one God and one mediator between God and men, the man Christ Jesus' (1 Timothy 2:5) and Jesus could not have made it clearer: 'I am the way and the truth and the life. No one comes to the Father except through me' (John 14:6). Jesus is not merely the *only* Saviour of sinners, he is the *exclusive* Saviour and you must trust him exclusively. It is impossible for Jesus to save you unless you come to him empty-handed. You must throw away your trust in everything else and cast yourself upon him alone. Jesus came into the world to save sinners; he died to save sinners; he lives to save sinners — and you are a sinner! *Then turn to him and be saved!*

2. Submit to Jesus and acknowledge him as your Lord

As we saw earlier, the gospel message is not merely a call to 'have faith in our Lord Jesus' but also to 'turn to God in repentance', and it is vitally important to grasp this. The first recorded words in the public ministry of Jesus were 'Repent and believe the good news!' (Mark 1:15), and these two commands are inseparable. Genuine faith always involves repentance, genuine repentance always involves faith, and both are equally important to salvation. We have already seen that the person who trusts Christ 'shall not perish but have eternal life', whereas the person who refuses to do so 'stands condemned already', and the Bible says the same things about repentance. The apostles called people to 'repent ... and turn to God, so that your sins may be wiped out' (Acts 3:19), while Jesus warned people of the alternative: 'Unless you repent, you ... will all perish' (Luke 13:3).

But what is repentance? It is turning from sin to God with a genuine and complete change of mind, heart and will. There is an excellent illustration of repentance in Psalm 51 where King David, racked with guilt because of his sin, finally comes to his senses and turns to God. He has a *change of mind*: 'For I know my transgressions, and my sin is always before me'(v. 3). He does not try to cover anything up, make excuses, or blame his circumstances. Nor does he play down his own sins by suggesting that at least he is better than some people. Instead, there is an honest, open acknowledgement of 'transgressions' (his sinful actions) and 'sin' (his depravity and corruption). He also has a *change of heart*: 'Against you, you only, have I sinned and done what is evil in your sight' (v. 4). David sees sin for what it really is, not just an unfortunate lapse, an error of judgement or a personal weakness, but rebellion against God, a violation of God's holy law and a personal insult to his majesty and honour — and when he realizes this he is broken-hearted and disgusted. He sees sin as something vile and loathsome, and he hates it. He also has *a change of will*: 'Have mercy on me, O God... Wash away all my iniquity and cleanse me from my sin... Create in me a pure heart, O God' (vv. 1,2,10). He longs not just to be forgiven but to be cleansed, not just for pardon but for purity, not just for the past to be dealt with but for the future to be different. He wants to lead a new life, one that is clean, upright, honest and pleasing to God.

True repentance is an open confession of sin, an earnest hatred of sin and a genuine longing to turn away from sin; and to those who truly repent the Bible makes this great promise:

> 'Let the wicked forsake his way
>   and the evil man his thoughts.
> Let him turn to the LORD, and he will have mercy on him,
>   and to our God, for he will freely pardon'
>   (Isaiah 55:7).

Yet we have already seen that we can only 'turn to the Lord' through Jesus Christ, who is the 'one mediator between God and men'. This means that just as we can only trust God to save us by trusting in Jesus, so we can only repent towards God by submitting to Jesus. Just as we come to God by coming to Jesus, find God by finding Jesus and trust God by trusting Jesus, so we are to obey God by obeying Jesus.

The call Jesus gives is a double-barrelled one: not just 'Come to me' (Matthew 11:28), but 'Follow me' (Mark 2:14). He calls us to receive something and to give something; to receive forgiveness from him and to give allegiance to him — and we cannot have one without the other. *He does not offer to forgive any sin that we are not willing to forsake.* Note that! Jesus calls for a radical change in our thinking and behaviour. When crowds were flocking after him, fascinated by his teaching and miracles, Jesus warned them that becoming a Christian was not a soft option. He told them to think carefully and to count the cost before committing themselves to him, warning them that 'Any of you who does not give up everything he has cannot be my disciple' (Luke 14:33). Nobody can accuse Jesus of putting his terms in small print. Everything was out in the open. Becoming a Christian brought forgiveness, peace with God and eternal life, but it also demanded repentance, self-denial and wholehearted obedience to Christ.

The terms have not changed. As Walter Chantry puts it, 'Jesus will not be Saviour to any man who refuses to bow to him as Lord.'[10] If you come to Christ you must fall down before him on the two 'knees' of faith and repentance. You must come to him not only confessing your sin and guilt and calling on him to have mercy upon you and save you, but acknowledging his right to rule every part of your life. In other words, becoming a Christian means trusting Jesus as your Saviour and taking him as your Sovereign. You cannot separate him into two parts and have one without the other, because 'in biblical terms there is no difference between having Jesus Christ as Saviour and having him as Lord'.[11] The preaching of the apostles was 'the good news about the *Lord* Jesus' (Acts 11:20). Paul's answer to the question, 'Sirs, what must I do to be saved?' was 'Believe in the *Lord* Jesus, and you will be saved' (Acts 16:30-31), and he told the Romans that 'Christ died and returned to life so that he might be the *Lord*...' (Romans 14:9). In Walter Chantry's words, 'This was no optional note on the apostolic trumpet. It was the melody, the theme of their instruction to sinners.'[12]

The challenge

All of this tells us that the gospel message is not the offer of an easy ride to heaven but a direct challenge to the will: God *commands* you to repent, to change your whole moral and spiritual direction. He calls for a revolution in your mind, heart and will. Are you willing for the revolution to take place? Do you honestly want a renewed mind, a clean heart, a holy will, a godly life? Are you prepared to have 'every thought' made 'obedient to Christ' (2 Corinthians 10:5)? Are you ready to abandon your self-centred independence and to place your thoughts, words and actions under his control? Are you willing for him to be in charge of your time, your work, your leisure, your money, your relationships — everything?

Perhaps you do want to turn wholeheartedly to Jesus as Saviour and Lord, but feel that you lack the power to believe or repent. If so, you have made an important discovery. You *are* powerless, either to trust Jesus or to obey him, *but God is able and willing to give you the power you need.* Paul tells the Christians at Ephesus, 'For it is by grace you have been saved, through *faith* — and this is not from yourselves, it is *the gift of God*' (Ephesians 2:8), while Peter says that Jesus has been exalted to heaven 'that he might *give repentance* and forgiveness of sins' (Acts 5:31). In other words, God not only commands your obedience, he gives you power to obey!

This means that nothing whatever need hold you back. God is willing to save you, 'not wanting anyone to perish, but everyone to come to repentance' (2 Peter 3:9). Then ask him to have mercy on you, to give you faith and repentance, and to save you. The responsibility to do this is entirely yours. What more can God say? He has spoken 'through the prophets at many times and in various ways' (Hebrews 1:1), and in the pages of Scripture has given us his 'living and enduring word'

(1 Peter 1:23). What greater sacrifice can God offer? He 'did
not spare his own Son, but gave him up for us all' (Romans
8:32). What greater love can God show? 'God demonstrates
his own love for us in this: While we were still sinners, Christ
died for us' (Romans 5:8). What greater promises can God
make? His 'very great and precious promises' (2 Peter 1:4)
include the forgiveness of sins, peace with God, eternal life
and the presence and power of the Holy Spirit to enable you to
live a new life. What greater warnings can God give? He tells
you that those who do not obey the gospel will be 'punished
with everlasting destruction and shut out from the presence of
the Lord and from the majesty of his power' (2 Thessalonians
1:9).

   In the light of all this, what is your response to 'the real Jesus'?
Here is the Creator and upholder of the universe, the eternal
Son of God, who stripped himself of his heavenly glory in order
to become a man, lived a life of perfect holiness, deliberately
went to a degrading death in order to bear the sins of others,
rose triumphantly from the dead and ascended to share again
his Father's glory in heaven, and now promises the forgiveness
of sins and eternal life to all who will trust him as their Saviour
and take him as their Lord. *What do you think of him? What
will you do with him?* If you reject all the evidence and decide
that he was demonic, deluded or demented, you will presumably have no qualms about closing this book and forgetting
him. That would be a horrific tragedy, and one that will be
made infinitely worse when you face him on the Day of Judgement and hear him say, 'Depart from me, you who are cursed,
into the eternal fire prepared for the devil and his angels' (Matthew 25:41). Imagine what it will be like to be sentenced by the
one who died to set sinners free, condemned by the one who
came to bring forgiveness, turned into hell by the one who came
to invite rebels to heaven!

Yet God's words to Israel in the Old Testament are equally true for you today: 'As surely as I live, declares the Sovereign LORD, I take no pleasure in the death of the wicked, but rather that they turn from their ways and live. Turn! Turn from your evil ways! Why will you die...?' (Ezekiel 33:11). So are the words of Jesus: 'Whoever comes to me I will never drive away' (John 6:37); 'Come to me, all you who are weary and burdened, and I will give you rest' (Matthew 11:28).

Then come to him now! Turn to him, trust him, fling yourself upon him, commit yourself to him, surrender your life to him. Cast yourself upon his mercy, his love, his grace, his power, and his willingness to save you. Listen to his words to the hesitant Thomas: 'Stop doubting and believe' (John 20:27); then fall at his feet in worship and cry, 'My Lord and my God!'

Postscript

If you have come to acknowledge Jesus Christ as your Saviour and Lord through the reading of this book, and would like help in beginning to read the Bible for yourself, you are invited to write to Dr John Blanchard, c/o Evangelical Press, Faverdale North Industrial Estate, Darlington, Durham, DL3 0PH, England, for a free copy of *Read Mark Learn*, his book of guidelines for personal Bible study based on Mark's Gospel.

If you need further help, please contact the following person:

Notes

Chapter 1

1. Because of some juggling with the calendar, the year dates now in universal use are not strictly accurate. Jesus was born 'during the time of King Herod' (Matthew 2:1) and fairly soon before Herod's death in the year 4 B.C. We can therefore add about five years to the 'A.D.' years; for example, the year 1989 is about 1994 years after the birth of Jesus.
2. Dr David Barrett, editor of *World Christian Encyclopaedia*, quoted in *Evangelical Times*, December 1987.
3. Wales is just under 7,500 square miles, about the same size as New Jersey, the fifth smallest of the United States of America.
4. The 1998 *Guinness Book of Records*.
5. Mission Aviation Fellowship.
6. K. S. Latourette, *Christianity in a Revolutionary Age*, Volume 1.
7. Cited by E. Stauffer, *Jesus and his story*.
8. L. Goppelt, cited by J. Piper, *Was Qumran the Cradle of Christianity?*

Chapter 2

1. John W. Wenham, *Christ and the Bible*.
2. Josephus, *Antiquities of the Jews*, XVIII.63-64. It has been suggested that the standard text of this passage includes phrases

Meet the real Jesus

Josephus would not have used, but which were added by a Christian editor. Even though there is no conclusive evidence for this, I have deliberately used the 'de-Christianized' version by Professor Joseph Klausner of the Hebrew University of Jerusalem, yet even this makes it clear that Jesus was a historical person.

3. 'Messiah' is the Hebrew word meaning 'the anointed One'. It is the equivalent of the New Testament word 'Christ'.

4. Josephus, *Antiquities of the Jews*, XX.200.

5. Suetonius, *Life of Claudius*, XXV.4.

6. 'Christ' is the Greek word *Christos*, meaning 'the anointed One'. It is the equivalent of the Old Testament word 'Messiah'.

7. Tacitus, *Annals of Imperial Rome*, XV.44.

8. F. F. Bruce, *Jesus and Christian Origins outside the New Testament*.

9. Pliny, *Epistles*, X.96.

10. As above.

11. Lucian, *The Passing of Peregrinus*.

12. There are numerous other contemporary and ancient references to Jesus outside the Bible, including Jewish, Christian and Islamic sources (the Koran has many references to him) but they would take too long to investigate and do not add any historically verifiable evidence.

13. Roderic Dunkerley, *Beyond the Gospels*.

14. All the biblical references to Jesus by name are obviously in the New Testament, and it will keep our investigation flowing if we concentrate on this. However, the evidence for the reliability of the Old Testament is equally impressive. When the Dead Sea Scrolls were discovered in 1947 they gave us 40,000 fragments of 500 scrolls of Old Testament manuscripts. These were dated about 1,000 years earlier than any we had previously possessed, and represented all or part of every Old Testament book except Esther. The measure of their agreement with older manuscripts was amazing. For example, in *A General Introduction to the Bible*, Drs Normal L. Geisler and William E. Nix show that in

one very important chapter in the book of Isaiah only one three-letter word is in question, and that it does not significantly alter the meaning of the passage. To give just one more example, in his book *A Scientific Investigation of the Old Testament*, Dr Robert Dick Wilson illustrates the astonishing accuracy of the transmission of Old Testament information about thirty-six kings reigning over various countries during a period of 1,600 years by saying that not even a single consonant was wrongly copied or translated and that the possibility of the accuracy being a fluke was one in 750,000,000,000,000,000,000,000,000!

15. Normal L. Geisler and William E. Nix, *A General Introduction to the Bible*.
16. Philip Schaff, *Companion to the Greek Testament and the English Versions*.
17. As above.
18. Frederic G. Kenyon, *Our Bible and the Ancient Manuscripts*.
19. Papyrus was a cheap kind of 'paper' made from the pith of the papyrus plant, which grew on riverbanks. It could easily be formed into rolls up to ten yards or so in length.
20. 'Codex' is the name for an early form of book, made by sewing together leaves of writing material. Codices were often made from papyrus or longer-lasting vellum.
21. Frederic G. Kenyon, *Handbook to the Textual Criticism of the New Testament*.
22. The Gospel of Mark is thought to be the first New Testament book to be written.
23. Eusebius, *Ecclesiastical History*.
24. i.e. the Jews.
25. i.e. their deaths.
26. This refers to an incident recorded at John 13:23-25.
27. Irenaeus, *Against Heretics III*.
28. As above.
29. i.e. the Latin professorship.
30. Sir William Ramsay, *St Paul the Traveller and Roman Citizen*.

31. Sir William Ramsay, *The Bearing of Recent Discoveries on the Trustworthiness of the New Testament.*

32. E. M. Blaiklock, *The Acts of the Apostles.*

33. Nelson Glueck, *Rivers in the Desert: History of Neteg.*

34. F. F. Bruce, *The Books and the Parchments.*

35. This is the New Testament's word for the Old Testament writings; it is now used of the Bible as a whole.

36. Harold Lindsell, *God's Incomparable Word.*

37. B. B. Warfield, *The Inspiration and Authority of the Bible.*

38. John M. Frame, Essay 'Scripture speaks for itself' in *God's Inerrant Word* (ed. J. W. Montgomery).

39. John Young, *The Case against Christ.*

40. Calvin had been speaking about God the Holy Spirit.

41. John Calvin, *Institutes of the Christian Religion*, Vol.1.

42. J. N. Geldenhuys, article 'Life of Jesus Christ' in *New Bible Dictionary.*

43. Albert Einstein, *Saturday Evening Post*, 26 October 1929.

44. Clark Pinnock, *Set Forth Your Case.*

45. Cited by Vernon Grounds, *Reason for our Hope.*

46. Cited in *The Encyclopaedia of Religious Quotations* (ed. Frank Mead).

47. Cited by Wilbur Smith, *Have you considered Him?*

48. In a message to the people of Israel, their great leader Moses had said, 'The LORD your God will raise up for you a prophet like me from among your own brothers. You must listen to him' (Deuteronomy 18:15).

49. R. Bultmann, *Jesus and the Word.*

50. I. Howard Marshall, *I Believe in the Historical Jesus.*

Chapter 3

1. Peter W. Stoner, Foreword to *Science Speaks.*

2. Stoner, *Science Speaks.*

3. As above.

Chapter 4

1. *Collins Concise English Dictionary.*
2. *The Times,* 13 July 1984.
3. C. S. Lewis, *Miracles.*
4. Henry Morris, *The Bible has the Answer.*
5. *Evangelical Times,* March 1985.
6. H. D. McDonald, *The God Who Responds.*
7. J. Gresham Machen, *The Christian View of Man.*
8. Alan Richardson, article in *A Dictionary of Christian Theology.*
9. Cited by Thomas Boslooper, *The Virgin Birth.*
10. Robert G. Gromacki, *The Virgin Birth.*
11. Cited by G. W. McPherson, *The Virgin Birth.*
12. A. Rendle Short, *The Bible and Modern Research.*
13. John Calvin, *Commentaries on the Epistles of Paul to the Galatians and Ephesians.*
14. Thomas Boston, *Complete Works,* Vol.1.
15. Douglas Edwards, *The Virgin Birth: History and Faith.*
16. As above.
17. Edward J. Young, *The Book of Isaiah.*
18. Matthew Henry, *Commentary on the Whole Bible.*

Chapter 5

1. There is also a New Testament book called 'James' but it is generally agreed that this was written not by the apostle but by another James, who was a brother of Jesus.
2. Thomas Manton, *The Epistle of James.*
3. John Calvin, *Opera Calvini.*
4. Augustine Burrell, *Miscellanies.*
5. Cited by Robert Clarke, *The Christ of God.*
6. D. M. Lloyd-Jones. Foreword to A. Dallimore, *George Whitefield.*
7. George Whitefield, *Whitefield's Journals.*
8. Ashbel Green, Discourses delivered in the College of New Jersey.

9. Cited by Iain Murray, *Jonathan Edwards*.
10. Cited by J. Oswald Smith, *David Brainerd*.
11. Clarke, *The Christ of God*.
12. C. E. Jefferson, *The Character of Jesus*.
13. D. M. Lloyd-Jones, *Darkness and Light*.
14. *New American Standard Bible*.
15. Michael Green, *Why Bother with Jesus?*
16. Clarke, *The Christ of God*.

Chapter 6

1. Leon Morris, *The Cross in the New Testament*.
2. Cicero, *In Defence of Rabirius*.
3. John R. W. Stott, *The Cross of Christ*.
4. Thomas Brooks, *The Works of Thomas Brooks, Vol.V*.
5. J. I. Packer, *God's Words*.
6. Derek Kidner, *Genesis: An Introduction and Commentary*.
7. Packer, *God's Words*.
8. Svetlana Alliluyeva, *Twenty Letters to a Friend*.
9. Cited by M. R. Vincent, *Word Studies in the New Testament*.
10. Robert Clarke, *The Christ of God*.
11. Albert Barnes, *Notes on the Old Testament*.
12. John R. W. Stott, *Basic Christianity*.
13. A. W. Pink, *The Attributes of God*.
14. Packer, *God's Words*.
15. John Calvin, *Commentaries on the Epistles to Timothy, Titus and Philemon*.
16. John Bunyan, *The Pilgrim's Progress*.
17. Geoffrey B. Wilson, *Romans*.
18. William Sanday and Arthur C. Headlam, *A Critical and Exegetical Commentary on the Epistle to the Romans* in *The International Critical Commentary*.
19. Packer, *God's Words*.

20. Morris, *The Cross in the New Testament.*
21. Bruce Hunt, *For a Testimony.*
22. The words Jesus spoke were in Aramaic. Mark has supplied the translation.
23. C. H. Spurgeon, *Metropolitan Tabernacle Pulpit, Volume 36: Sermon preached on 2 March 1890.*
24. R. B. Kuiper, *The Bible Tells us So.*
25. G. Campbell Morgan, *The Crises of the Christ.*

Chapter 7

1. Paul Althaus, *Die Wahrheit des kirchlichen Osterglaubens.*
2. W. E. Vine, *Expository Dictionary of New Testament Words.*
3. Kersopp Lake, *The Historical Evidence for the Resurrection of Jesus Christ.*
4. Norman Anderson, *Jesus Christ: the witness of History.*
5. As above.
6. Some commentators think that the guard set at the tomb was Jewish, not Roman, but the evidence seems against this. The point is not crucial; in either case the guard would have been sufficient to prevent any removal of the body.
7. Malcolm Muggeridge, *Jesus Rediscovered.*
8. Andrew Fairbairn, *Studies in the Life of Christ.*
9. Justinian, *Digest* 49.16. The same kind of argument applies if the guard was Jewish, where the penalty for sleeping was death by burning.
10. John R. W. Stott, *Basic Christianity.*
11. J. Duncan M. Derrett, *The Anastasis: The Resurrection of Jesus as an Historical Event.*
12. James Montgomery Boice, *God the Redeemer.*
13. Stott, *Basic Christianity.*
14. Chrysostom, cited by J. C. Ryle in *Expository Thoughts on the Gospels.*

15. Stott, *Basic Christianity.*
16. Vine, *Expository Dictionary.*
17. Ethelbert W. Bullinger, *A Critical Lexicon and Concordance to the English and Greek New Testament.*
18. J. A. Alexander, *A Commentary on the Acts of the Apostles.*
19. Stott, *Basic Christianity.*
20. W. H. Griffith Thomas, *The Principles of Theology.*
21. William Milligan, *The Resurrection of our Lord.*
22. Leon Morris, *The Tyndale New Testament Commentaries: The Gospel According to Luke.*
23. A. Rendle Short, *Why Believe?*
24. J. Gresham Machen, cited by E. F. Kevan, *The Resurrection of Christ.*
25. D. M. Lloyd-Jones, *Romans: The New Man. An Exposition of Chapter 6.*
26. Celsus, *The True Doctrine.*
27. J. Glyn Owen, *From Simon to Peter.*
28. Anderson, *Jesus Christ: the witness of History.*
29. Michael Green, *Man Alive!*
30. K. S. Latourette, *A History of the Expansion of Christianity*, Vol.1.
31. Milligan, *The Resurrection of our Lord.*
32. Vine, *Expository Dictionary.*
33. E. G. Robinson, *Christian Theology.*
34. Frank Morison, *Who Moved the Stone?*
35. As above.
36. S. Greenleaf, *An Examination of the Testimony of the Four Evangelists by the Rules of Evidence administered in the Courts of Justice.*
37. Cited by Wilbur M. Smith, *Therefore Stand: Christian Apologetics.*
38. Cited by Green, *Man Alive!*
39. Cited by Stott, *Basic Christianity.*
40. C. S. Lewis, *Miracles.*

Chapter 8

1. C. S. Lewis. *They Stand Together: The Letters of C. S. Lewis to Arthur Greeves.*
2. J. C. Ryle, *Expository Thoughts on the Gospels.*
3. John W. Wenham, *Christ and the Bible.*
4. James Montgomery Boice, *God the Redeemer.*
5. C. K. Barnett, *The Gospel According to St John.*
6. Josh McDowell and Bart Larsen, *Jesus: A Biblical Defense of His Deity.*
7. Philo, *Life of Moses: iii.41.*
8. C. E. B. Cranfield, *A Critical and Exegetical Commentary on the Epistle to the Romans.*
9. Albert Barnes, *Barnes' Notes on the New Testament.*
10. B. A. Milne, article on 'Salvation' in *The Illustrated Bible Dictionary.*
11. G. Campbell Morgan, *The Categorical Imperatives of the Christian Faith.*
12. Paul Tournier, cited in *Reader's Digest*: January 1967.
13. C. S. Lewis, *Mere Christianity.*
14. John Brown, cited by Arthur W. Pink, *Exposition of the Gospel of John.*
15. *The Book of Common Prayer*: The Order of the Administration of the Lord's Supper or Holy Communion.
16. William Hendriksen, *A Commentary on the Gospel of John.*
17. R. V. G. Tasker, *The Tyndale New Testament Commentaries — The Gospel According to St John.*
18. Benjamin B. Warfield, *The Person and Work of Christ.*
19. Ignatius, *Letter to the Ephesians.*
20. Tertullian, *De Carne Christi.*
21. Gregory of Nazianzua, *Orat, xlv 22.*
22. John Brown, *An Exposition of the Epistle to the Hebrews.*
23. Warfield, *Person and Work of Christ.*

24. J. A. Motyer, *The Richness of Christ: Studies in the Letter to the Philippians.*
25. J. I. Packer, *Knowing God.*
26. Campbell Morgan, *Categorical Imperatives.*
27. As above.

Chapter 9

1. R. P. Martin, Article 'Blasphemy' in *The Illustrated Bible Dictionary.*
2. William E. Lecky, *History of European Morals from Augustus to Charlemagne.*
3. Cited by Herbert Dandy, *The Jew and Christianity.*
4. *Un Souvenir de Solferino.*
5. K. S. Latourette, *A History of Christianity.*
6. C. S. Lewis, *Mere Christianity.*
7. Norman Anderson, *Jesus Christ: the witness of History.*
8. John W. Wenham, *The Goodness of God.*
9. R. V. G. Tasker, *Tyndale New Testament Commentaries: The Gospel According to St John.*
10. Walter J. Chantry, *Today's Gospel: Authentic or Synthetic?*
11. T. Alan Chrisope, *Jesus is Lord.*
12. Chantry, *Today's Gospel.*

Printed in the United States
54149LVS00002BA/1-135

9 780852 344996